Lady Margaret Douglas: Countess of Lennox

A Tudor Times Insight

By Tudor Times

Published by Tudor Times Ltd

Tudor Times Insights

Tudor Times Insights are books collating articles from our website www.tudortimes.co.uk which is a repository for a wide variety of information about the Tudor and Stewart period 1485 – 1625. There you can find material on People, Places, Daily Life, Military & Warfare, Politics & Economics and Religion. The site has a Book Review section, with author interviews and a book club. It also features comprehensive family trees, and a 'What's On' event list with information about forthcoming activities relevant to the Tudors and Stewarts.

Titles in the Series

Profiles

People

Politics & Economy

Contents

Lady Margaret Douglas: Countess of Lennox

Introduction

Lady Margaret Douglas, Countess of Lennox was the niece of Henry VIII, and both aunt and mother-in-law of Mary, Queen of Scots. Exiled at a young age from her native Scotland, Margaret was a great favourite at the English court, with a wide range of friends, both Catholic and Protestant. Imprisoned in the Tower three times, for '*matters of love*', as she put it, but really at least twice for furthering her ambitions, her life is a microcosm of Tudor intrigue.

Lady Margaret spent her childhood in Scotland and the borders before being housed in the palaces of the English court. During her married life, she spent the majority of her time in the great houses that Henry VIII had granted her – that is, when she was not in the Tower of London!

This book contains Lady Margaret Douglas' Life Story and additional articles about her, looking at different aspects of her life. Lady Margaret's life encompassed almost every experience a sixteenth century princess could have, with the exception of execution or coronation. She was a lady-in-waiting to Queens, mistress of great estates, mother of eight children, a prisoner, a wife, and even a poet.

Family Tree

Lady Margaret Douglas
Countess of Lennox

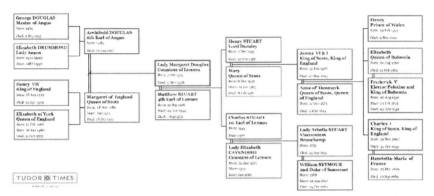

TUDOR ✖ TIMES

Lady Margaret Douglas' Life Story

Chapter 1: A Dramatic Birth

Lady Margaret Douglas was born on 7th October (not 8th, as in some sources) 1515, at Harbottle Castle in Northumberland. Her mother, Margaret Tudor, Dowager Queen of Scots, and Countess of Angus, widowed after the Battle of Flodden in 1513, had been deprived of her position as Governor of the Realm during the minority of her son, James V, when she married Margaret's father, Archibald Douglas, 6th Earl of Angus.

Angus, described by his uncle, Gavin Douglas, as a *'young, witless fool'*, was head of the powerful 'Red' Douglas clan, based at Tantallon Castle, and generally inclined to the pro-English party in Scotland, rather than the majority pro-French grouping. He failed to mention to Queen Margaret before their marriage, that he was already pre-contracted to marry Lady Janet Stewart of Trequair, an issue that came back to haunt both him, and his daughter.

The other Scottish nobles resented the match, believing it would lead to Angus dominating the government and invited the Duke of Albany, the young King's closest male heir, to return to Scotland from his home in France to take up the role of Governor. Queen Margaret felt hounded when she was forced to relinquish her sons and her fears were stoked by Thomas, Lord Dacre, the English Warden of the East March. Dacre requested instructions from Queen Margaret's brother, Henry VIII of England, in a letter of 7th September 1515 on what to do with Queen

Margaret if their negotiation with her to leave Scotland should succeed *'as we trust verily it shall, to the great disturbance of all Scotland'*.

Eventually, Queen Margaret was persuaded to take refuge over the border and, leaving Linlithgow in secret, arrived at Harbottle a few days before her first child by Angus was due. Lady Margaret's birth was difficult, unsurprising in the circumstances. Nevertheless, she thrived, and was christened on 8th October, with Cardinal Thomas Wolsey (represented by a proxy) named as her godfather.

The fact that Lady Margaret Douglas was born in England had an important long term effect on her position. Born in England of an English mother, she was treated as an English subject, and thus eligible to inherit the Crown. A Statute of Edward III prohibited inheritance to individuals born out of the realm, although there were doubts as to whether this applied to the Crown.

Queen Margaret was very ill with sciatica following Margaret's birth. She lay immovable, barely able to sit up in bed. In the meantime, it was rumoured in Europe that Henry intended to invade Scotland. His minister, Cardinal Wolsey, maintained that there was absolutely no English intention whatever to invade Scotland, or France. Nevertheless, he added menacingly, if Albany did not mend his ways with reference to Queen Margaret, Henry would be forced to make him. Albany continued, with little success, to reach an accommodation with the Queen.

After some to-ing and fro-ing of letters, it was decided by Henry and his Council to invite Queen Margaret and her husband, Angus, south for Christmas. In the event, the party did not travel to London in November, perhaps because of Queen Margaret's continued frailty or because Henry had not yet decided on the best policy with reference to Scotland. Instead, Queen Margaret and the baby Margaret were moved in very slow stages of four or five miles each day to Morpeth, which had a few more of the creature comforts to which the Queen was accustomed, arriving on

23rd November 1515. They were met there by Angus, who appears to have returned to Scotland in the period after the original arrival at Harbottle.

Henry finally made arrangements for Queen Margaret and the baby Margaret to travel south, planning that they should set out from Morpeth on 7th April, and furnishing them with a litter and attendants. Mother and daughter set out on 8th April 1516, accompanied by Dacre and others, travelling first to Newcastle, where they were met by Sir Thomas Parr and then on to Durham.

Queen Margaret was no doubt thrilled to be travelling south at last, but, at the same time, she was in 'much heaviness' as, a couple of weeks earlier, Angus had resolved to return to Scotland and make his peace with Albany. Whether the Queen's unhappiness stemmed from a sense of betrayal, or because she missed him, we cannot know. She would have understood Angus' need to keep his estates that were threatened with forfeiture, and, when she knew that Angus' return was inevitable, she wrote to Albany asking him to restore to Angus the castles of Tantallon and Bothwell. Henry was more condemnatory and characterised Angus' actions as 'done like a Scot'.

Whether Angus was sorry to leave Queen Margaret is another question. On his return home, he quickly renewed his relationship with Janet Stewart of Traquair, who, in due course delivered a daughter, known as Lady Janet Douglas. He chose to set up home with Lady Janet in Queen Margaret's own dower castle in Newark, a fact which, when it came to her notice, enraged her far more than the simple matter of adultery.

Queen Margaret and the young Margaret continued to travel slowly towards London. On 3rd May, they entered London at Tottenham, as was traditional for Scots Ambassadors, before travelling to Greenwich, where the court was rejoicing in the birth of Mary, a live child at last, to Henry and Katharine, following at least four previous unsuccessful pregnancies.

Chapter 2: Scottish Years

Henry VIII saw his sisters first and foremost as a means to take and retain power for his dynasty. His view was that a Scottish regency favourable to England was an outcome to be promoted by whatever means possible. At this time, even after the live birth of Mary, it was looking increasingly likely that Henry's nearest male heir would remain the young king of Scots: a most unwelcome prospect to Henry.

At the very least if he could influence the boy through his mother, and, ideally, have him brought to England, the prospect might not be so bad. To achieve this, he needed Margaret in Scotland, not idling her time away at his expense in Westminster. Finally in December 1516, the terms of a treaty were agreed that would permit Queen Margaret to return to Scotland.

Queen Margaret and Lady Margaret, now eighteen months old, set out from London on 18th May 1517 in some state. On 15th June they were met at Berwick by Albany's deputy. Angus was also waiting for them at nearby Lamberton Kirk, and, ignorant as yet of the existence of Lady Janet of Traquair and her daughter, Queen Margaret was delighted to see him. Queen Margaret took up residence at Holyrood Palace, and, presumably, Lady Margaret was with her. The rapprochement between Queen Margaret and Angus did not last long, and Queen Margaret was soon writing to her brother.

'Also, please you to wit that I am sore troubled with my lord of Angus, since my last coming into Scotland, and every day more and more, so that we have not been together this half year.'

So far as is known, Margaret remained with her mother, but there are no records of her upbringing or education during this period. Late in 1517, Queen Margaret began to wonder if she could have her marriage to Angus annulled, but was persuaded against the idea at that time. By 1520, Margaret's parents were again on good terms, but by 1521, the relationship had broken down completely. In that year Angus, who had tried to undermine Albany's regency, was exiled to France.

Eventually, Angus travelled to England, where he was well-received by Henry, and began an alliance with his brother-in-law which required him to promote English interests in Scotland. Henry seems to have got on well with Angus, apparently preferring him to Queen Margaret, and certainly ignoring all her complaints about him.

Many writers have accepted the theory that Angus took Margaret with him to France, and then to England. However, this seems unlikely, as no mention of it is made in the records (we could fairly infer that Queen Margaret would have made huge protests to her brother). A letter that purports to date from 1524 from the Queen, complaining that Angus had kept her child from her for the preceding three years, should probably, according to the records in the *Douglas Book*, be dated to 1528. Margaret's most recent biographer, Alison Weir, concurs with this and believes that Margaret remained with her mother until at least 1525, although it is possible she was at one of Angus' castles, perhaps Tantallon, or with his other family.

Wherever Margaret was, there is no record of her education, but some information can be gleaned from later records, and the customs of the time. She would have learnt to read, and probably, but not necessarily at this time, to write. Her later writings are all in English, whereas one must suppose that during this period of her life she would have spoken Scots (Scots is a Germanic language, which developed in parallel with English from Anglo-Saxon languages, not be confused with Gaelic, the

Celtic language of the West and the Highlands). It seems likely that Lady Margaret would also have had at least some understanding of French, which was widely spoken at both the Scots and English courts.

If Margaret were brought up away from her mother, it is likely she would have been educated as was usual for young noblewomen, with an emphasis on the practical skills of running a great household - a woman of Margaret's rank would have been expected to be able to care for the estates of her future husband. It is unlikely that at this point Angus would have had any ambition for her beyond marriage to one of his fellow peers.

If Margaret remained with her mother during these years, she might have profited from a more sophisticated education such as her own mother had received, with perhaps a smattering of Latin and history. Wherever she was educated, she would certainly have been taught to sing, and probably play the lute and the virginals. Plenty of physical exercise would have been part of daily life - riding, hunting and possibly falconry.

She would also have been brought up to practise traditional forms of religion. In this regard Margaret remained loyal to the teaching of her childhood and did not move with the times. She remained an adherent of the Catholic Church throughout her life. The veneration of images and relics and undertaking of pilgrimages was as widely-practised in Scotland as elsewhere, although amongst the intellectuals of Europe these practices were being laughed at and questioned as hinting at idolatry. This scepticism did not rub off on Margaret, who was later noted as a great lover and collector of relics.

Chapter 3: Exile

After Angus was exiled in 1524, Queen Margaret requested the Pope for an annulment (although the term 'divorce' is used) on the grounds of Angus' prior betrothal to Lady Janet of Traquair. Back in England, Henry, Katharine and Wolsey were scandalised by her action, and exerted themselves to prevent it in every way. Wolsey wrote to Henry explaining his efforts at hindering the matter, as it was feared that the Queen intended to marry Albany, with whom she was rumoured to be having an affair.

In 1524, Queen Margaret persuaded the Scots Estates to declare that the regency of Albany was at an end, and that King James should now rule himself. On this, Angus returned to Scotland where he continued to make trouble for his wife and step-son. He seized James and for the next three years dominated Scottish government. His daughter's whereabouts are not known for certain, but she was probably kept close to her father's side, and thus in near proximity to her half-brother in the various royal palaces at Stirling, Linlithgow or Edinburgh Castle. In early 1525 a betrothal between Lady Margaret and the Earl of Moray, the illegitimate half-brother of Margaret's own half-brother, King James, was suggested, but it came to nothing.

Queen Margaret's divorce was finally granted by the Pope in 1526 and pronounced in Scotland by Cardinal James Beaton, Archbishop of St Andrew's with the proviso that, as Queen Margaret had undertaken the marriage in good faith, the daughter of the union was legitimate. The Queen then married Henry Stewart, Lord Methven, described by the French Ambassador, du Bellay as '*a still finer fellow than himself (Angus)*'. There is no record as to what Margaret thought, if anything, about her step-father. James V treated him with contempt.

In 1528, James escaped from Angus and his brother George, and declared the whole Douglas family as '*proscribed*' and subject to forfeit of their lands. He apparently excluded his half-sister from this, but Angus chose to interpret it as including her, and took her with him to Tantallon. James, fearful that she would be taken to England, and anxious for her return, sent scouts the length of the border to hunt for her and bring her back to her mother, where an appropriate establishment was being provided for her.

Rumours of further marriage plans arose – this time to an even more inappropriate husband – James Stewart, Captain of Doune, the brother of Queen Margaret's third husband. The idea that James Stewart had been Queen Margaret's lover before her marriage to his brother hardly seems credible, but the teller of the tale, Alexander Pringle, was a retainer of the Douglas family and no doubt could hardly find a good word to say of Queen Margaret. At any rate, he gives this mooted marriage as the reason for Angus being eager to take Lady Margaret out of the country.

James marched south with some 8,000 men to besiege Tantallon, but Angus had already left and proceeded to undertake a series of skirmishes and sieges against his King during the period of October 1528 to May 1529. On 9th October, having avoided being captured by James at Coldingham Priory, Angus sent Margaret for shelter to King Henry VIII of England's border castle of Norham. It is not clear whether she actually went to Norham, and stayed there, or returned to her father. She is next heard of in 1529, at Berwick Castle, in the care of Thomas Strangeways, Captain of Berwick.

Unsure what to do with her, Strangeways sent Carlisle Herald to Wolsey for instructions, keeping her in the meantime in some level of confinement, probably to prevent her being captured by James and Queen Margaret (or rescued, depending on Margaret's point of view, which we do not have). Wolsey, no doubt harassed by his own problems of Henry's annulment, found time to send instructions to Strangeways to keep Lady Margaret and look after her as well as possible, whilst not permitting her to leave. Strangeways replied in July 1529, pointing out that he had already had the lady in his care for three months, without any money to provide for her.

'*Mr. Carlisle the herald hath declared to me that I shall keep still with me, in my house, the Lady Margaret, the daughter of the Earl of Angus ; and further, that I should take good heed to be sure of her ; but that she might hove as much liberty and recreation, and rather more, than she hath had. Please your Grace, even so according to your commandment sent me by the said herald, rightso I have used her before that commandment came to me. I was warned that if I took not good heed, and looked surely to her, she would be stolen and withdrawn into Scotland, which caused me to take more labor for her sure keeping; and yet I know well she was never merrier or more pleased and content than she is now, as she ofttimes repeats. My Lord of Angus, at the first bringing of her to me, desired that I would take her to my house, and he would content me both for her and for her gentlewomen, with such folk as wait upon her daily or resort to her. And I showed again to my said lord, that forasmuch as I understood that your Grace [Wolsey] was godfather to her, and seeing that my Lord of Angus was not provided with a convenient place for her to be in, I was content to take her, and do her the best service that might lay in my power, till such time as I knew your Grace's pleasure. Since the coming to Berwick of the said herald, I have showed my Lord of Angus that your express commandment to me by the said herald was, that I should keep and retain my lady still; wherewith he was very glad, and joyous that your Grace had his in such remembrance. An' it like your Grace, I have had the said lady and her gentlewomen, and a man-servant, with other of her friends and servants, at certain times, and for the most part the Earl of Angus her father, now by the space of three months, without any manner of costs to my said lord or any of them ; and what your Grace shall further command me in this matter, or any other, I shall be ready to accomplish the same by the grace of God.'*

The gentlewoman referred to is named as Isobel Hoppar who was married to Angus' uncle, another Archibald Douglas, so was probably more of a governess than a servant.

Chapter 4: Life in England

On 6th April 1530, Henry VIII paid for clothes for Margaret, but her actual whereabouts are not clear. There is a theory, supported by her latest biographer, Alison Weir, that she was sent from Northumberland to the household of her aunt, Mary, the French Queen at Westhorpe Castle in Suffolk. This is based on the content of a commemorative poem written about Margaret after her death, probably by a man who knew her. There are no contemporary records and other historians (Rosalind K Marshall, and William Fraser who collated the Douglas papers) place her immediately at Beaulieu with her cousin, Mary. In August of 1530, Strangeways requested 200 marks for the '*bringing-up*' of Lady Margaret, but the implication is that she had left his care.

By Christmas 1530 Margaret was at court and received £6 13s 4d to '*disport*' herself from Henry VIII. This gift was repeated the following year. Margaret was now in the retinue of her cousin, Mary, who was still treated as a Princess, her parents' marriage, although in dispute, not yet annulled. She would not, of course have remembered her cousin whom she had last seen in 1517, but the two girls struck up a friendship that lasted for the rest of Mary's life.

The cousins, some six months apart in age, were in the care of Mary's Lady Mistress, Margaret Plantagenet, Countess of Salisbury, cousin of their maternal grandmother, Elizabeth of York. Life in the Princess's household would have been closely regulated. At this time, Lady Salisbury was in her late fifties and likely to have been traditional in her approach to the upbringing of young ladies of the royal family. This would have been counterbalanced by the very modern education that Mary was receiving, although there is no evidence that Margaret shared her lessons. In total, there were 162 members of the household. Following Lady Salisbury in importance was Margaret herself, then ten other ladies and gentlewomen. Margaret received an annual salary of £10.

The girls spent most of their time at Mary's houses of Beaulieu and Hundson in Essex, with visits to the King and Queen at court at Easter and Christmas. They would also have seen Henry and Katharine as they moved around the various palaces on the north of London.

In their spare time the girls would have ridden, hunted, hawked and danced; played cards – in particular a game known as cent, similar to modern picquet, tables, chess and bowls and gambled on the outcome. Gambling was a permanent feature in Tudor entertainment. Mary remained a frequent gambler all her life, and Margaret presumably followed suit. There is no description of Margaret known at this age.

Henry gave both Angus and his brother George large sums of money to pay spies and undermine the Scots government, as well as for living expenses. The maintenance of Angus, his brother and daughter was set on a surer footing than random gifts of money when Henry granted the Earl a pension of £1,000 per annum in 1532. This was a munificent sum.

There is a record of a magnificent present of clothing for Margaret, her two gentlewomen and her servants in October 1531. The gift included three gowns of 11 and a half yards each – one of 'tynsen' (tinsel or some sort of gold cloth), one of black velvet, furred with powdered ermine and one of black damask, together with kirtles and sleeves (which were separate garments) of crimson satin, black satin and black velvet, each being seven and a half yards. More yards of white satin, black velvet and crimson satin for other items, 30 ells of Holland cloth (a type of high quality linen) for underclothes, two French hoods (the curved hoods set back on the wearer's hair familiar from paintings of Anne Boleyn), 12 pairs of hose, 6 pairs of black velvet shoes for indoor use, and six of leather, lacing ribbons and garters, 12 pairs of gloves, a lb of thread, 100 needles, 2 brushes and a '*standard*' 1 and three quarter yards, by ¾ of a yard. Presumably this last had her coat of arms on it and would have been carried in front of her when she travelled. In addition, there was a generous allowance of clothing for her servants.

Margaret's reaction to this sumptuous gift is not recorded, but what adolescent girl would not have been delighted at such a present, particularly if she had inherited her mother's love of '*rich apparel*'?

Clothes were not just pretty or useful items in themselves, they were also one of the most significant indicators of rank or status. With little in the way of consumer goods and in a pre-industrial age with nothing to invest in, other than land, wealth was displayed by your clothes and jewels. The mediaeval sumptuary laws which had striven to prevent men '*aping their betters*' and hence threatening the all-important hierarchy, were re-affirmed, and even strengthened, during the Tudor period. Certain colours, such as purple, and fabrics, such as cloth of gold, could not be worn other than by royalty or the highest ranks of nobility. Interestingly, the sumptuary laws did not generally apply to women. This gift of expensive fabrics, such as tynsen and velvet, showed Margaret's high rank and the generosity with which Henry treated her.

Chapter 5: At Anne Boleyn's Court

In 1533, when Princess Mary was demoted in rank, and had her household disbanded, Margaret was summoned to court to serve the new

Queen, Anne Boleyn, in the capacity of Chief Lady of the Bedchamber to Anne's recently born daughter, Elizabeth. It is not recorded whether Margaret was required to swear to the Acts of Succession and Supremacy in 1534, the former of which stated Henry and Katharine's marriage to be null and establishing Anne as his wife and Elizabeth his only legitimate child; the latter, repudiating the authority of the Pope, or Bishop of Rome as he was henceforth referred to. It seems highly likely that as the King's niece and in her position as First Lady of the Bedchamber to Elizabeth she would have been required to do so.

Nor is it apparent whether she joined Elizabeth's household in fact, as well as name. In March 1534, she is recorded as being at court, when the French Ambassador reported that Henry was offering Margaret as bride for François I of France's son, in place of the previously requested Mary.

'He [Henry] added that there were many other girls in his kingdom, and that he had a niece, daughter of the queen of Scotland, whom he keeps with the Queen his wife, and treats like a queen's daughter, and if any proposition were made for her, he would make her marriage worth as much as his daughter Mary's. I assure you the *lady* is beautiful, and highly esteemed here'

Henry and Katharine's court had always been magnificent. With Anne at his side, Henry continued to enjoy a wide variety of activities – gambling as always, but even astronomy. Anne, though not so well educated in a formal sense as Katharine, was undoubtedly a clever woman and seems to have had a biting wit which, whilst it made her many enemies who came back to haunt her, yet must have made her company exhilarating. However, wit was not enough for a Queen – she needed allies and friends – an '*affinity*' as it was called, and Anne was doing her best to create one.

The appointment of Lady Margaret Douglas, the King's own niece, daughter of a Queen, and half-sister of a King, to be her lady-in-waiting must have seems quite a coup, especially as it would separate Margaret from Mary, as Anne, perhaps jealous, but certainly frightened of Henry's lingering affection for his daughter, took every opportunity to undermine her and detach any of Mary's friends or supporters from her side. In addition, to have such a highly-born attendant would raise the tone of her household, and be some counter to the barely concealed contempt of the older court ladies – even her aunt, the Duke of Norfolk's wife, had refused to serve her, protesting her support of Katharine.

Amongst the circle of gentleman surrounding Anne, were the sons of the new gentry class that was rising under the Tudors, to the disgust of the older families, who complained of these 'new men'. Their charm for the King was that they had no power base or affinity of their own, and were completely dependent on him for favour. The new circle of friends included men such as Anne's father, Sir Thomas Boleyn and Henry Norris, the King's closest companion since his old friend and brother-in-law, Suffolk, was less supportive of the divorce than Henry would have liked.

The ladies of Queen Anne's household were a mixture of her personal friends, largely drawn from the daughters of her mother's twenty siblings and half-siblings, and, for state occasions, the great ladies who were the wives of the highest ranking nobles. Amongst these women, Margaret was to find her friends. Many of Anne's ladies were, like Anne, on the more evangelical wing of religious thought. This is hardly surprising, as conservatives rejected (in their hearts, even if not openly) the divorce and would not be clamouring to serve her, so taking an evangelical view was likely to gain favour with Anne. For Margaret, however, this does not seem to have been a problem. Her two closest friends at this time appear to have been Anne's paternal cousin Mary Shelton, and Mary Howard, the Duke of Norfolk's daughter, who was shortly to marry the King's illegitimate son, Henry Fitzroy, Duke of Richmond. Both of these ladies, and particularly Mary Howard, were later considered as evangelicals.

However, during the early 1530s religious difference had not yet hardened into the irreconcilable divide of Catholic and Protestant. In any event, although religion played a central role in the day to day life of everyone, young women in the sixteenth century enjoyed music, singing, dancing, poetry and thoughts of love just as much then, as they do now and they had ample opportunity to indulge these tastes at Anne's court.

Writing love poetry was a popular pastime amongst the erudite youth of the court and it was fashionable for lovers to write verse conversations and for poems to be written down and shared amongst friends, with each adding an answer to the previous poem. A large group of verses is contained in a manuscript, now known as the Devonshire manuscript, a collection of 183 poems, transcribed mainly in the hands of Margaret Douglas and Mary Shelton with various marginalia and comments - not always flattering to the versifiers - and in this document is a series of poems attributed to Margaret herself and her lover, Lord Thomas Howard.

Chapter 6: Courtship

By 1535, Margaret was 20 years old. This was an unusually advanced age for a noblewoman not to be married. The tentative arrangements that Queen Margaret had made for her ten years before had come to nothing, and there did not seem to be any definite prospects for her, despite the conversation with the French Ambassador.

Margaret, perhaps inheriting the romantic streak of her mother and uncle, was not content to wait, and sometime during late 1535 began a relationship with Lord Thomas Howard. Lord Thomas was the much younger half-brother of the Duke of Norfolk, with whom he confusingly shared his Christian name. Perhaps with twenty previous children, his father had run short of inspiration! Lord Thomas was some four years older than Margaret and had been honoured by Henry in being permitted to hold the canopy of estate over the baby Elizabeth at her christening. At Christmas, Howard and Margaret exchanged gifts - he gave her a cramp ring which was a fairly common gift amongst friends, and she gave him a miniature of herself.

It has been said that to begin with, Henry and Anne encouraged the match. This is based on the evidence of Queen Margaret's later letter in which she says that Henry had '*advised*' the match, however, the word advised at that time could also mean 'been informed of'. Nevertheless, there is no definite evidence that Henry was aware of the young couple's relationship at the time.

For Queen Anne, it would definitely be a welcome prospect. Any closer ties that Anne could make between her family and the King's would be to her advantage, and Henry, still eager to promote his second marriage as valid, and to raise Anne up in public estimation, would also have seen the benefits. Lord Thomas' elder brother, Lord William Howard had been dispatched in 1534 as Ambassador to Scotland where he proceeded to develop good relations with Queen Margaret who was now influential in her son's government. Margaret, as well as being in love, would have been well aware that marrying the Queen's uncle would be a good match for her.

In a complete volte face from Henry, Anne was disgraced, degraded from her rank and executed all within a period of weeks in Spring 1536. In the aftermath of Anne's execution, and the annulment of a marriage that apparently was not valid for an unspecified reason, Henry was left with two illegitimate daughters, an illegitimate son, and the offspring of his sisters. The numbers of possible claimants to the throne was reduced by the death on 31st May of Henry Fitzroy.

The Act of Succession of 4th July 1536, passed after Anne's death had the effect, surely not Henry's ideal scenario, of making Margaret his lawful heir, James being excluded as born out of the realm. The actual wording of the Act conferred the succession on the children of Henry's new queen, Jane Seymour (whose train Margaret had held at her wedding), but since she was not even pregnant at this time, logically, in default of Mary or Elizabeth, had Henry died before Jane became pregnant, the Crown would have devolved on either James V or Margaret Douglas. At this point, Henry woke up to the fact that his niece was embroiled in some sort of love affair that had previously had his tacit acceptance, and for Margaret, her betrothal to Lord Thomas was now a source of danger. Fortunately, the match had not been consummated, which would have created a binding marriage.

On the 9th July, the members of the former queen's household were questioned. Howard admitted to the relationship between himself and Margaret, saying they had been married *de verbi di praesenti*, but consummation had not taken place. Both Howard and Margaret were clapped in the Tower and an Act of Attainder was raced through Parliament against Howard, being both introduced and passed on the same day – 18th July 1536. An Act of Attainder permitted the execution without trial of an individual accused of treason. Instituted in the early 1530s they became Henry's weapon of choice for disposing of recalcitrant relatives who had undertaken activities that, not criminal at the time, but that Henry, in the aftermath, disapproved. Howard was convicted of an attempt to

' interrupt ympedyte and lett the seid Succession of the Crowne' .

The act imposed the death sentence on Howard and also forbade the marriage of any member of the King's family without his permission. Margaret was not included in the Act, and it was believed that the non-consummation of the marriage saved her.

Bizarrely, Sir Francis Bigod, who led the final phase of the uprisings around the Pilgrimage of Grace in early 1537, claimed in his statement that it was commonly supposed that the Act of Attainder against Thomas Howard had been instigated by Cromwell, as he wished to marry Margaret himself. It is hard to believe any credence could be given to such a rumour.

Chapter 7: Imprisonment

The sentence was not carried out immediately and Thomas and Margaret remained in the Tower throughout the summer of 1536. The example of Anne's death must have thoroughly frightened Margaret. She could not suppose that nearness of blood to the King would save her, but she perhaps put her hope in her parents or half-brother to plead for her with Henry. There is no record of Angus taking any action, although of course he may have done, but on 12th August 1536, Queen Margaret wrote an importunate letter to her brother, first marvelling that since he had known about the betrothal earlier, he could then punish her daughter for carrying it out.

She followed this by begging him, both for affection for herself, and respect for King James to allow Margaret to be sent back to a Scotland, so that *in time coming she shall never come into your Grace's presence.* Henry, however, had no intention of letting such a useful bargaining chip slip from his grasp and the young couple remained in prison.

It need not be thought that Margaret was confined to a gloomy dungeon, lying on straw watching the damp creep down the slimy walls and listening to the scurrying of rats in the straw. That indeed, was the fate of many prisoners, but nobles confined to the Tower were held in the upper rooms, usually in the Bell Tower or the Lord Lieutenant's own quarters. Margaret probably had her gentlewomen and servant to wait upon her, and might even have received guests. That her captivity, although frightening, was not rigid, is supported by the likelihood that she and Thomas were exchanging verses whilst in confinement. Lord Thomas appears to have been more faithful than Margaret, who eventually renounced his love. One can hardly blame her, aged 21, urged to obey her uncle the King. She would also have had in mind the shocking death of her former mistress, Anne, and many of Margaret's circle and perhaps the scene of it before her eyes, out of her prison window.

By 20th October, 1536, Margaret's mother wrote to Henry, thanking him for his '*nobleness*' towards her daughter, and confirming that she would never give her blessing to her wayward child if she did not conform to the King's will. From this we may infer that Henry had pardoned Margaret.

There is a difference in historians' accounts as to what happened next. Wriothesley's Chronicle, a contemporary document, suggests that Margaret remained in the Tower until the end of October 1537. This is the view taken by Alison Weir in her recent biography, who also cites a letter from Queen Margaret of 30th October 1537, saying how pleased she is that Margaret is no longer in the Tower. Ms Weir then notes that Margaret was conveyed to Syon Abbey by barge on 24th November 1537 and that she was at the Abbey for convalescence, rather than under house arrest.

A contrary view, is that Margaret left the Tower in November 1536, for conveyance to Syon. This rests on a letter from the Abbess of Syon that confirms she is willing to take Margaret into the precinct of the convent. The letter is catalogued in the '*Letters and Papers of the Reign of Henry VIII*' and also in the collection of letters transcribed in 1822 as '*Letters of Illustrious Ladies of Great Britain*' as pertaining to November 1536. However, Ms Weir contends that this is a misplacement, and that it should be placed in November 1537. The earlier date would seem to accord with Queen Margaret's letter of 20th October 1536 and Henry's response to it in December 1536 that although Margaret had '*used herself to her dishonour'*, yet, in future, if she behaved, Henry would be good to her. This seems to imply that she had been forgiven and it was in that month that she received from him the gift of a magnificent crimson velvet chair, with 2,000 nails and silver fringe at 5s the ounce. Chairs were the preserve of the highest ranks, and this specimen must have been a splendid example. Would Henry have sent such a present if she were still in the Tower and would she have been kept there for a further ten months after being forgiven?

Furthermore, there is a letter from Margaret, again transcribed in *Letters of Royal and Illustrious Ladies of Great Britain*. Letters and Papers catalogues it in August 1536, with which Ms Weir concurs, giving it as written from the Tower. The transcription in *Royal and Illustrious Ladies* also dates it to 1536, but with no month given. It could be argued that the text, although the tone of it suggests that Lord Thomas is still alive, is more consistent with Margaret being at Syon for a couple of reasons: first, it refers to a complaint by Cromwell about her keeping excessive numbers of servants and having too many visitors. It is hard to believe that, imprisoned in the Tower, she could have had excess servants or visitors. Second, Margaret denies that her servants are an additional charge to the 'house' and uses the expression 'house' twice, which might seem an odd way of referring to the Tower. The letter may be found at page 61.

Wherever Margaret was, Lord Thomas continued to languish in the Tower. Eventually, he fell ill, and before Henry could either confirm his execution, or release him, he died on 31st October, 1537. Margaret apparently took Lord Thomas' death hard, despite her protestations to Cromwell, and one of the last entries in the Devonshire Manuscript from her is a long poem with a definitely suicidal tone. Suicide was the most terrible sin of all, and it is unlikely a woman of Margaret's apparent energy and spirits would have contemplated such a terrible step for long, but the verses make sombre reading. Margaret was unable to mourn publicly for Lord Thomas. His mother, Agnes, Dowager Duchess of Norfolk was granted permission by the King to take his body and bury it

'so [on the condition] that she bury him without pomp.'

Lord Thomas was interred, with many others of the family, at Thetford Priory.

That Margaret was ill both during, and after, her time in the Tower is attested by medical expenses paid by the King, to the tune of £14 4s. Henry also paid £20 to Dr Cromer, possibly for medical services, but more likely for spiritual advice, as the payment is for *'preparations against Easter.'* There seem to be two Drs Cromer – one a physician, and the second a priest who had preached on Palm Sunday, and who was later accused of heresy. It is possible, of course, that they were one and the same.

There is no record of Margaret leaving Syon or where she went, although there is a note from Cromwell to pay her expenses there in April 1538. As the court was in mourning for Jane Seymour, it seems likely she returned to the household of her cousin, Mary, and she was certainly there by June 1538.

Chapter 8: Queen's Lady

In October 1538, Margaret was again mentioned as a possible spouse for a foreign prince. Henry suggested that, if the Emperor Charles accepted Mary for his protégé, the Infante of Portugal (Charles' nominee for the Duchy of Milan) Henry would allow Charles to choose suitable Italian princes for Margaret, the Lady Elizabeth, and the widowed Duchess of Richmond – a case of buy one get three free! Again, the negotiations went nowhere.

Henry began to look for a new wife for himself and, his choice falling on Anne of Cleves, a new household was formed for her. Margaret was to be the chief of the *'Great Ladies'*, and she was also to be part of the welcoming committee for the new Queen at Blackheath in late 1539. In recognition of her status, she was given one of the best apartments at Hampton Court.

Another of the ladies in the new Queen's service was Mistress Katheryn Howard, who was the half-niece of Margaret's former lover. She was probably about five years younger than Margaret, and far below her in rank, so it must have come as a shock to Margaret when Katheryn replaced Anne of Cleves as Queen in August 1540. Whatever her thoughts, Margaret kept them to herself, retaining a position in the Royal Household, and being given a gift of *'beads'* (a rosary) by the new Queen.

Just as Queen Katheryn's cousin, Anne Boleyn, had surrounded herself with cheerful young cousins and friends, so did Katheryn. Among her household were her various siblings, including Charles Howard, with whom Margaret struck up a flirtation. It was now three years since Thomas Howard's death, and probably four since she had actually seen him. Aged 25, it was more than time for Margaret to marry, but no plans were forthcoming.

In October of 1541, Margaret's mother, Queen Margaret, died. She requested that her goods be given to Margaret, since she had never previously given her anything but James V kept them for himself. It was some fifteen years since Margaret had last seen her mother, and there is no record of correspondence between them, but that does not, of course, mean that she did not grieve. But a more immediate worry was soon upon Margaret – the King had been informed that his pretty young wife was not chaste, and immediate enquiries began.

Katheryn Howard was arrested and sent first to Syon, then to the Tower, on charges of adultery. Margaret would have been questioned with the rest of her ladies, but was not implicated in the Queen's bad behaviour. Queen Katheryn's household was broken up on 11th November 1541, with an instruction that Margaret was to go to Kenninghall, in Norfolk, the property of the Duke of Norfolk. She was to go with her friend, Mary, Duchess of Richmond, Norfolk's daughter and widow of Henry's late illegitimate son. The Privy Council note says that she is to be sent there if *'my lord her father and she are content.'* This requirement has generally been read to refer to Norfolk and Mary because Margaret was in disgrace, but could be read to mean Angus and Margaret - suggesting that Margaret had some choice in the matter. This view may be supported by the fact that Norfolk was one of the signatories. He must have known whether he was *'content'* or not. It also seems unlikely that Mary Richmond would have been asked for her opinion.

It is only the following day, after further examinations of the Queen had taken place, that Cranmer was told to take a stern message to Lady Margaret, rebuking her for acting indiscreetly, first with Lord Thomas, and now with Charles Howard. Cranmer was to tell her to *'beware the third time.'*

Margaret appears to have stayed with the Howards at Kenninghall for some time, writing to her father from there in October 1542. She may have visited Lady Mary at Christmas 1542, when she gave the Princess a carnation velvet gown for New Year, although in Lady Mary's accounts there is a tip for Margaret's servant for delivering it. She herself would have been in mourning that Christmas – her half-brother, King James V of Scotland died in early December 1542, after a defeat at the Battle of Solway Moss. There is no reason to suppose that Margaret was personally grieved by James' death. He was the cause of her original exile to England and his personal hatred for her father, Angus had never wavered, but, of course, we do not know the state of her emotions. Angus had fought for the English at the Scots victory at Haddon Rig, immediately before Solway Moss, but the Anglo-Scots landscape now changed dramatically with James' death.

The new Scots Regent, the Earl of Arran, although head of the Hamiltons, who were enemies of the Douglas clan, was pro-English, and in favour of a policy of Church reform. He made overtures towards England, and Henry, seeing the possibility of English domination of Scotland through the marriage of his son, Edward, to the baby Queen of Scots, encouraged Angus to return to Scotland to further the match. This seemed a good plan to Henry, who let Angus travel north. Angus was restored to his lands, sworn to Arran's Privy Council, and married to Margaret Maxwell, all within a few months.

On 12th July, 1543, Lady Margaret was one of the witnesses of Henry VIII's sixth marriage, to Katherine Parr, the widowed Lady Latimer. The new Queen was a good friend of the Lady Mary, and was soon surrounded by many faces familiar to Margaret – Mary of Richmond; Anne Stanhope, Countess of Hertford; Katherine Willoughby, Duchess of Suffolk. All four of these women, and the Queen herself, were evangelists in religion, unlike Margaret or Lady Mary, but that does not seem to have caused problems.

In February 1544, Margaret, described as the *'Princess of Scotland'* was noted as one of the ladies of the Queen's suite who welcomed and entertained the Duke of Najera. She danced with various gentlemen, and, at the end, all of the English ladies were kissed by the Duke.

Having been bridesmaid to at least two, probably three, of Henry's queens, it was now Margaret's turn to be married at last.

Chapter 9: Marriage Negotiations

It is impossible to know when Margaret first heard a marriage mooted between herself and Matthew Stuart, 4th Earl of Lennox, but Henry's Council and her father were negotiating for it from July of 1543. Lennox had spent most of his youth in France, where he was an important figure in the Scots Guard around François I. He had left Scotland in the wake of his father's murder by one of the Hamiltons. This shared enmity for the Hamiltons and their leader, the Earl of Arran, was a link with Angus, but in 1543, with Angus reconciled to Arran as Governor of the Realm, it looked as though the two would be on opposing sides. Lennox returned to Scotland with the view of ousting Arran from the Governorship – a role he felt belonged to him, as, in his view, his claim to be the young Queen Mary's heir was superior to Arran's.

Lennox represented the French alliance, and hoped to marry Marie of Guise, the Dowager Queen. She held him off, but gave him enough encouragement for him to help her in her plan to move to Stirling to enable her daughter to be crowned.

At some point, Arran turned away from Henry, and dismissed the idea of the marriage between Mary and Edward, reconciling more fully with the Queen Dowager and Cardinal Beaton, the other leader of the pro-French party. The bitterness between Arran and Lennox was so strong that this influenced the latter to turn towards the English party. Arran had stated quite clearly that he would not be of the same party as Lennox, unless the latter recognised his right as 'second person of the realm'. Lennox, claiming that place for himself, refused to do so and presumably was determined to be on any side against Arran. Marie de Guise began to suspect that Lennox, would betray the Governor and herself and warned Arran (who needed no prompting) against trusting him.

By the end of October 1543, Lennox was at Dumbarton Castle, whence a French loan of 10,000 crowns together with munitions, a Legate from the Pope, and the French Ambassador had been sent. Queen Marie told the Venetian envoy that she would have preferred the gold to be at '*the bottom of the sea*' rather than that it should fall into Lennox' hands.

Marie was right in her surmise that Lennox would betray her, as he was now in secret negotiation with the English, and was demanding, as part of his price for betraying Dumbarton to Henry's men, that not only should he marry Margaret, but that they should succeed her father, Angus, in the Earldom of Angus, even though Angus had sons by his third marriage. Angus refused to agree to this. The Dowager, Cardinal and Governor all commanded Lennox to send the money, munitions, Legate and Ambassador to Edinburgh. Sir Ralph Sadler (Henry's Ambassador) believed Lennox might send the latter two, but would hang on to the useful items. The Venetian envoy could not believe that Lennox, being a '*Lord and a Gentleman*', would so dishonour himself, and risk the loss of the King of France's favour as well as his lands in France and expectation of more there: however it seems that Lennox's hatred and jealousy of Arran and his resentment at his rejection by Marie were stronger than his loyalty to the King of France. Whilst Henry considered his proposals, Lennox temporised with Marie, promising, but failing, to deliver the money and munitions to her.

By March of 1544, it appeared that Henry had agreed in principle to the marriage, although he made the caveat that the young couple must agree to it, once they had seen each other, as he had promised his niece '*never to cause her to marry any but whom she shall find in her own heart to love*'. This is less likely to be a reflection of Henry's romantic streak, than a loophole for breaking the match off if he changed his mind.

Chapter 10 Countess of Lennox

On 26th June, 1544, Henry and Lennox entered a treaty for the marriage. In return for Lennox abandoning his claims to the Scots throne in favour of Henry, giving up his French estates, and betraying Dumbarton and Bute to the English, he was to receive Lady Margaret Douglas in marriage, and a handsome estate. Also listed in the treaty were the lands that Margaret was to have from Lennox as her jointure, which were part of the Lennox earldom and amounted to 500 marks Scots per annum. When Henry achieved his fantasy of overlordship of Scotland, Lennox would be Governor under him, and could take any revenue over the cost of running the country and maintaining Margaret. He was also to cause the *'Word of God'* to be preached in Scotland. As Henry was still firmly Catholic in doctrine, we may suppose that this was merely to reiterate Catholic teaching, with the rejection of Papal authority.

The signing of the treaty was celebrated with a feast at which Henry, Lennox, Prince Edward and the Ladies Mary and Elizabeth were present. Margaret herself is not named, although she may have been there.

Three days later, on 29th June 1544, at St James' Palace, Margaret married Lennox after Mass, with the King and Queen in attendance. There is no record of Margaret's initial reaction to the marriage, but we can assume that she would have been pleased, for a number of reasons, not least the fact that she was close to thirty in an age which considered the appropriate age for women of her class to be married was about twenty. The fact that Lennox himself was the same age as her, and by all accounts a personable man, was unlikely to have escaped her.

Margaret is likely to have been warmly disposed to the match for political reasons too. She was a strong supporter of Henry's policy, still being pursued by her father, Angus, of the marriage of Edward and Mary Queen of Scots. Such a match would have made her aunt-by-marriage to the next King of England, as well as cousin – never a bad idea to be closely allied to the Crown, provided that one's loyalty was not suspect.

Henry's motives for keeping Margaret single so long are likely to have been similar to his reasons for keeping his daughter, Mary, single. Apart from wanting to hang on to his bargaining chips as long as possible, he was reluctant to provide either woman with a husband who might challenge either Henry himself, or more likely, the young Edward, should Henry die before Edward was able to hold his throne firmly. He must have been strongly convinced either that Lennox would be loyal, although a talent for loyalty had not been conspicuously demonstrated by Lennox' behaviour to date, or that the English would be so solidly against a Scottish King that he would not pose a threat. Lennox became a 'denizen' of England – that is, he swore allegiance to the English King.

On her wedding, Margaret received a generous gift of jewellery from the Lady Mary consisting of several gold brooches with diamonds, sapphires and emeralds.

Henry granted Margaret and Lennox vast swathes of land in Yorkshire. To fulfil the marriage treaty, their value had to be at least 6,800 marks Scots, or 1,700 marks English – about £1,100 English. The lands were made up of property from the Percy Earldom of Northumberland, the lands of dissolved monasteries, including that of Jervaulx, and land confiscated from rebels after the Pilgrimage of Grace. The lands were granted to the couple jointly, and entailed on their joint heirs – ensuring that, in the event of Margaret's death without heirs, they would not pass to the children of any subsequent wife of Lennox. The extent of their lands made them the second largest landowners (excluding the Crown) in the whole of the north, next only to Henry Clifford, Earl of Cumberland, married to Margaret's cousin Eleanor Brandon.

Margaret was now a Countess with vast estates. The lands they received were:

- Temple Newsam
- Temple Hurst
- Settrington
- Whorlton
- Kirk Leavington,
- Breighton
- Grange of Rookwith
- Abbey of Jervaulx together with land in Feldum and Didderston, and 6 carucates in Hutton Hang and the manor and land at Elington
- Scrafton, Caldbergh, Carlton, Arundel House and Slape Gill, with their five respective granges, which had belonged to Coverham Abbey

Chapter 11: Early Married Life

The complexities of the political relations between England and Scotland in the last years of Henry's reign are too great to cover here in detail – more can be found in the Profile of Marie of Guise. Suffice to say, that Lennox continued to support Henry's policy. Henry VIII was determined to get his money's worth from Lennox, and during much of the next few years Lennox was raising armies and spending time in Ireland and Scotland to promote the English cause in the War of the Rough Wooings. On 1st October 1545 at Linlithgow, the Scots Parliament convicted Lennox of treason and confiscated his lands.

During her husband's absences, Margaret seems to have remained at court. She was with Queen Katherine during September 1544, when Henry sent greetings from Boulogne to her, and is recorded as present at the visit of the French Ambassador to Hampton Court in August 1546. Although she is named in precedence after the Ladies Mary, Elizabeth and Anne of Cleves, it does not seem that she was '*pricked*' (chosen) to sit at the feast.

Nevertheless, Lennox and she met sufficiently frequently for her to have borne and lost a son, Henry, Lord Darnley, by November 1545, and to have a second in the following month, also named Henry. In all, Margaret was to have eight children, four daughters and four sons. There are no records of the daughters' names, or dates of birth or death, so they presumably died in infancy. Her last two sons, Philip and Charles were born in the mid-1550s, but only Henry and Charles reached manhood.

Not long before Margaret's marriage, the Third Act of Succession had been passed, which laid down the succession to the English Crown – first Edward, then Mary, then Elizabeth, with a proviso for Henry to name Elizabeth's successors (should she have no children) in his will, or by Letters Patent. This act overturned the common law, both by permitting the inheritance by two women who were, under English law, illegitimate, and by allowing the King to specify an heir who might not be the heir under common law.

Under the usual rules of inheritance, on the assumption that Mary and Elizabeth were both illegitimate, then Henry's heir was Edward, followed by Margaret's niece, the baby Queen of Scots, or, if, as was sometimes claimed Queen Mary was debarred from the Crown by foreign birth, Margaret herself. As in 1544 it was probably assumed that at least one of the King's children would have an heir, it seems unlikely that Margaret considered herself to have been wronged, especially as she probably considered that at least Mary was legitimate. She may even have thought that Henry might name her in his will to follow Elizabeth. It was not until the King, in his final will, named as Elizabeth's successors the children of Margaret's other cousin, Frances, Duchess of Suffolk, that Margaret knew herself to have been definitely passed over.

It has been speculated that Margaret had quarrelled with Henry, and that was the reason he cut her out of the succession, but there is no evidence to support this. It is far more likely that, despite his personal fondness for her, Henry could not countenance Lennox as King of England – it being assumed that any woman inheriting would naturally be subordinate to her husband. It may also have been the result of Angus finally abandoning Henry and the English alliance (see next chapter).

On Henry's death, Margaret and Lennox moved north, basing themselves at Temple Newsam, near Leeds where they concentrated on managing their estates.

As Edward's government introduced more reformist legislation it appears that Margaret became known for retaining Catholic practices, although she must have conformed sufficiently to keep within the law. Lennox' religion seems to have been a more fluid affair. He was probably Catholic in such convictions as he may have had, but had no trouble with working with Protestants in Scotland. Their sons, Henry, Lord Darnley, and Charles Stuart were brought up as Catholic, but Darnley also appears to have been willing to be flexible on religion.

During Edward's reign, the Lennoxes did not often travel to court, although Margaret was one of the great ladies who entertained the Regent of Scotland, Marie of Guise on her journey from France to Scotland, via England in November 1551.

Chapter 12: Quarrel with Angus

As noted earlier, on Angus' return to Scotland he had married Margaret Maxwell, and had at least three children by her, although only one, James Douglas, survived childhood. In August, 1547, Angus arranged for transfer of his lands to James, retaining only a life-interest, but young James died early the following year.

Angus continued in Henry's pay until June 1546, when the Scots Parliament rejected the Treaty of Edinburgh which had been agreed by Arran for the marriage of Queen Mary and Prince Edward. On 22nd August 1546, Angus, and his brother, Sir George Douglas, swore allegiance to Arran as Governor. Margaret's father and son were now on opposing sides. There can be no doubt that Margaret's loyalties lay with Lennox and the pro-English party. Henry, as may be imagined, was beside himself with the loss of the Scots marriage, and continued to try to bring it about by force. After his death, Edward's Lord Protector, the Duke of Somerset, maintained the war, during which Lennox burned Annan on 8th September 1547, a raid that was swiftly followed by the Battle of Pinkie Cleugh. Pinkie, at which Angus fought for Scotland, was a disastrous defeat for Scotland, but Somerset was unable to follow it up with any long term control.

Later that year, Angus wrote to Margaret, asking her to plead with the English government for kind treatment for his illegitimate son, (another George) and other hostages who had been taken by the English. The Lennoxes were not inclined to help, and did not intervene to any effect. Despite his efforts, Lennox was not a successful commander, and the English never managed to gain mastery of Scotland. Eventually, the young Mary, Queen of Scots was sent in secret to France, and the pro-French party continued to rule the country until the crisis of 1559-1560.

Angus was hoping to improve his relationship with Margaret and Lennox, promising the latter some hawks, and sending letters that were loving and affectionate – dwelling on his love for Margaret and his desire to see her, and, by implication, her son, young Lord Darnley.

Margaret was not impressed. She was furious with her father, both for his perceived disloyalty to the pro-English party, and, more importantly, his actions with regard to her inheritance. In the land arrangement mentioned above, Angus had entailed the earldom of Angus to 'tail male' – that is, in default of sons of his own line, the earldom would pass to his next male heir – at that time his brother, Sir George Douglas. This disinherited Margaret, as the Earldom of Angus had previously been heritable by women. On 15th March 1549, Margaret wrote one of the sternest letters of the period from a child to a parent. In it, she points out that George Douglas couldn't wait for Angus to die, so that he could inherit, but that if Angus had no more sons and she were passed over, 'many a man shall smart for it'.

The full text of the letter is set out at page 61, as it is very illustrative of Margaret's character.

She also mentions that she plans to visit Carlisle, but there is no record of whether she did or not. In April 1552, there is a mention in the Privy Council of her as wishing to return home, as she is pregnant, although whether home means Scotland or Temple Newsam is not specified. Margaret does seem to have visited Scotland in 1552, perhaps for the first time since leaving back in 1528 and she probably visited Angus at Tantallon. Even if they were reconciled during this visit, Angus did not change the entail on his lands, and a dispute over inheritance flared up after his death.

Whilst the exact dates of Margaret's visit are unknown, what is clear is that Lennox and her children were retained in England. Ms Weir postulates that the visit was advantageous to the English government as it kept Margaret out of the way during the summer of 1553, when an attempt was made to put Lady Jane Grey on the throne in place of the Lady Mary.

LADY MARGARET'S LIFE STORY

Chapter 13: Second Lady in the Kingdom

Whether or not Margaret was out of the country when her cousin and friend, Mary, acceded to the throne, she certainly made haste to travel to London, secure in the knowledge that she would be welcomed. She was present at court on 17th October 1553 when the new Imperial Ambassador, Simon Renard arrived. Later in the year, the French Ambassador, de Noailles, reported that the Countess of Lennox, spoken of as '*My Lady Margaret*' and also Frances, Duchess of Suffolk, were sometimes given precedence over the Queen's half-sister, the Lady Elizabeth.

Margaret, whose son, Henry, Lord Darnley was now about 8 years old, seems to have seen Mary's reign as the opportunity both to promote Darnley as a possible male heir, and also to enlist the new Queen's support for Lennox' campaign to have his Scottish estates restored.

Mary certainly favoured the Lennoxes – the Earl was granted the position of Master of the Queen's Hawks, and Margaret received valuable clothes and jewellery. Darnley was the lucky recipient of some of the late King Edward's clothes, and also his lutes. Mary herself was a notable lute-player, so Margaret was probably pleased to see that Darnley's skill impressed the Queen.

It should be noted, however, that Mary also showed high favour to Edward Courtenay – the son of the Marquess of Exeter, who had been executed in 1538. Courtenay had been in the Tower since that time, sent in as a child, and now emerging as a possible suitor for the Queen. She dismissed that prospect, but, as a great-grandson of Edward IV, Courtenay had a very respectable claim to the throne himself.

Mary was determined to provide her own heir, and quickly decided to marry Philip of Spain. This caused some disquiet amongst the Protestant faction and rebellion flared up in Kent and the Midlands. The Duke of

Suffolk and Courtenay were both implicated, but, as Courtenay's confession before the event had allowed the government to prepare and defeat the rebels, he was pardoned and exiled. Suffolk and his daughter, Lady Jane Grey, were executed and the Lady Elizabeth, who was suspected of complicity, was sent to the Tower. It was later claimed that Margaret had encouraged Mary to imprison Elizabeth, and perhaps to have her executed as well. Whether true or no, there does not seem to have been much love lost between Margaret and Elizabeth.

When the marriage of Mary and Philip finally took place in July 1554, at Winchester, Margaret acted as the Queen's train-bearer. Following the wedding, Margaret, although pregnant again, remained at court, acting as Mary's chief Lady-in-waiting. During Mary's reign, Margaret bore two sons, Philip and Charles, but only the latter survived.

In early 1557, Margaret's father, the Earl of Angus, died. She immediately claimed the earldom, and signed her letters as Margaret, Countess of Lennox and Angus. The difficulty was, that she was in England, and the Angus lands were in Scotland, being taken possession of by Archibald Douglas, grandson of her uncle, Sir George.

Queen Mary wrote to the Scottish Regent (now Marie of Guise, in place of Arran, or Chatelherault, to give him his new title) requesting her to support Margaret's claims. Marie sent a gracious response with reference to the Angus lands but refused to have anything to do with trying to overturn the forfeiture of Lennox' lands, saying it was a matter to be decided by her daughter, Mary Queen of Scots herself. As the said Queen was in France, and still only fourteen, this was obviously intended as a rejection. More discussions were held over the Angus lands later that year, but to little avail, from Margaret's point of view.

Queen Marie was more helpful towards the end of 1557, agreeing to further discussions on the matter, but it remained unresolved.

A slight embarrassment occurred for the Lennoxes when the Earl's brother, John Stuart, who held the French estates and titles of Aubigny, was captured, fighting for France at the Battle of St Quentin – a major victory for the allied Anglo-Spanish army. Having been ransomed, he then proceeded to fight for France at the siege of Calais, the loss of which broke Queen Mary's heart, and then to take part in border raids from Scotland. Lennox and his brother were in continued communication. Such consorting with her enemies must have raised Mary's suspicions about the trustworthiness of Lennox, and perhaps of Margaret, but no action was taken against them before Mary's death in November 1558.

Chapter 14: Suspicion

On Queen Mary's death, Margaret performed her last duty as the Queen's friend and lady-in-waiting, acting as Chief Mourner at the funeral in Westminster Abbey. She also played a part in the coronation of the new Queen, Elizabeth, although she did not have the coveted office of train-bearer. But once these duties were done, Elizabeth made it quite clear that Margaret was not welcome at her court. Elizabeth disliked all her royal female relatives and certainly did not wish to give any hint that Margaret or her son could be considered as possible successors.

The Lennoxes moved further north from Temple Newsam, spending time at their properties in Settrington, and Jervaulx, in areas of the country that the Reformation had barely touched. The Act of Uniformity of 1559 required all subjects of England to attend the Anglican service in their parish church, however, it exempted gentlemen with private chapels. It was thus possible for the Lennoxes and many others of the nobility to continue to hear the Catholic Mass. There seems little doubt that Margaret did so, and also brought her sons up in the old faith.

The Elizabethan world was awash with spies and informers – Elizabeth and Cecil had paid informers in the Lennox household, and Margaret had spies in the Queen's court. Everyone was spying on everyone else, till it becomes impossible to know where anyone's loyalties actually lay. In the Lennox household was one Thomas Bishop. He had been secretary to Lennox before his marriage, but had fallen out with Margaret to the extent that he was dismissed. He held a permanent grudge against her for this, and, although Lennox had taken pity on Bishop when he was destitute and reinstated him, he repaid his employer by spying on the family and reporting, with the blackest possible spin, everything they said and did to Elizabeth's government. Much of the information on the Lennoxes comes from this source, so should perhaps be taken with a pinch of salt.

There was continuing turmoil in Scotland. Marie of Guise was being challenged by the Lords of the Covenant who wished to institute Protestantism as the state religion. To counter them, she made overtures to Lennox, promising restoration of his estates, and also that Margaret would be confirmed in the Earldom of Angus. The Lords of the Covenant requested the English government to refuse Lennox licence to leave the country.

Margaret, with two sons, was looking to the future – in the eyes of many Catholics, including herself, Elizabeth was illegitimate. Nothing in Margaret's behaviour suggests that she sought directly to overthrow Elizabeth, but she clearly wanted her son to be recognised as heir. However, England was not the only possibility for Darnley. There was also the prospect of re-establishing him in Scotland, as Earl of Lennox and Angus, and, should the Queen of Scots not bear an heir (she was married to the young King of France, François II) then he had a claim to that throne too, through his father. Twelve year old Darnley was sent to France, at the urging of Lennox' brother, Aubigny, to congratulate

François and Mary on their accession and request the return of the Lennox estates. Queen Mary was gracious, but refused the request.

Lennox, whilst ostensibly conforming to Elizabeth's policy of supporting the Lords of the Covenant, showing the government letters he had received from Aubigny, was also communicating secretly via the French Ambassador with Marie of Guise, furnishing him with a family tree, showing that the Lennox claim to be Mary, Queen of Scots' heir was superior to that of the English backed Chatelherault's.

This soon got the Lennoxes into trouble – the Council summoned them to London, and Margaret was questioned. Elizabeth's council also began to look into the matter of Margaret's legitimacy – claiming that the divorce that Queen Margaret Tudor had obtained, back in 1527, on the basis of Angus' pre-contract to Lady Janet of Trequair, rendered Margaret illegitimate. On the surface however, Elizabeth continued to support Lennox' claim to his lands.

Despite this, Darnley was being openly talked of as a possible to successor to Elizabeth, who was beset on all sides to confirm the succession. She would not name Lady Katherine Grey, the preferred Protestant choice, and she certainly would not name Mary, Queen of Scots or Darnley, both of whom were Catholic, and likely to be controlled (in the English view) by France.

Before long, the Scottish throne looked as though it might come a little closer. Francois II died in December 1560, leaving Queen Mary childless – perhaps young Darnley, now 14 to the Queen's 18, might make a suitable second husband, uniting their claims to the English throne, and strengthening the throne of Scotland?

Chapter 15: Plotting the Darnley Marriage

As soon as Queen Mary was known to be widowed, it was immediately assumed in both Scotland and England, that the Lennoxes would try to arrange her marriage to Darnley. Simultaneously, Chatelherault was hoping she would marry his son, James Hamilton, Earl of Arran, who was also a possible suitor to Elizabeth. Margaret wrote letters to Queen Mary, which were delivered in person by Darnley, who had been allowed by Elizabeth to go with her own Ambassador to offer condolences. Mary, however, was far more interested in a match with Spain, and paid little attention to the young man.

In August of 1561, Mary, Queen of Scots returned to take up personal rule of her kingdom. This completely negated any requirement for a regent (Marie of Guise having died) and so that immediate bone of contention between Chatelherault and Lennox was removed, although they still vied to be nominated as her heir. On the Queen's return, Lennox again petitioned for reinstatement of his lands, but Mary prevaricated. Thomas Bishop, the man noted above as Margaret's enemy, told the English government that Margaret was regularly communicating with her niece, and perhaps giving her more information about happenings in England than should have been shared with a foreign ruler.

Margaret was certainly promoting the idea of a marriage between Queen Mary and Darnley at this time, and Queen Mary later said that she had been pestered with endless letters, messages and presents.

In November 1561, Margaret and her children were summoned to London. The Catholic Earls of Northumberland and Westmoreland were similarly called for. The Spanish Ambassador, de Quadra, reported that Margaret feared arrest, and was determined to defend her actions by saying that the marriage of Mary and Darnley would avert civil war, in the event of Elizabeth's death without heirs. It does not appear that

Margaret obeyed the summons, although what excuse she sent is unrecorded.

Margaret was also accused to the Council of seeking to prevent a meeting between Mary and Elizabeth, on the grounds that she was afraid Mary would let slip information about their correspondence. However, it is absolutely clear that Elizabeth's government, Cecil in particular, did not want Elizabeth and Mary to meet, and, if Margaret did warn Mary that to leave Scotland would risk the English capturing her capital, she probably had truth on her side – the English government was continuing to support the Lords of the Congregation against their lawful Queen, although more subtly than previously.

Queen Mary, of course, was far more interested in being named Elizabeth's successor directly, than embroiling herself with the Lennoxes, and was quite willing to inform Elizabeth's council about her dealings with them.

In January 1562, Margaret was horrified to hear that Lennox had been arrested in London and was being held at the home of the Master of the Rolls. He had travelled to London to explain some rather unfortunate missives to Scotland that had fallen into the hands of the government. Thomas Bishop, who had once again been sacked by the Lennoxes, who accused him of spreading malicious lies about them, outdid himself in his accusations against them – everything from consulting astrologers to cowardice on the part of Lennox, and illegitimacy on the part of Margaret.

There was no help forthcoming from Scotland – Queen Mary had no interest at this stage in Darnley or his parents. Another of the Lennox servants was questioned – Francis Yaxley, who seems to have been at one time a confederate of William Cecil and sat for Stamford in the 1555 Parliament (Cecil's own borough). However, whether he was a spy for the English government throughout his service to the Lennoxes, or whether he just confessed everything he could think of to save himself, will never be known. In any event, he confirmed that he had, on Margaret's behalf, been seeking to arrange the marriage of Darnley to Queen Mary.

Following this, Lennox was removed to the Tower and Margaret was arrested at Settrington and brought to London, where she was placed under house arrest with Sir Richard Sackville, in the old Charterhouse at Sheen.

Chapter 16: Serious Charges

The government now discovered that the Spanish Ambassador, de Quadra, had been fomenting a plot to put Margaret on the throne in place of Elizabeth, claiming there would be widespread support for her, if King Philip would but send help. There is no evidence that Margaret knew anything about this, but she had been in correspondence with de Quadra. Thomas Bishop, and his colleague, William Forbes, another spy in the Lennox household, now gave statements to the Council, listing a long series of potentially treasonable activities by Margaret, including witchcraft (apparently, the striking of St Paul's by lightening was her doing!) hearing Mass and conspiring to overthrow the Queen.

Margaret, unaware of these damning charges (whether or not they were true) began to write importunate letters to Cecil, on her husband's behalf, begging the Queen to either release him from the Tower, or at least give him more liberty within it – it seems Lennox struggled with some sort of sleeping disorder or fear of being left alone that made prison particularly hard for him. No response was made to these pleas.

In late May, the Council came to Sheen to interrogate Margaret. She steadfastly rejected all that Bishop and Forbes had deposed, asking them to be brought to face her, and requesting permission to see Elizabeth.

She was particularly hot under the ruff about the accusation that she was illegitimate. Questioning of other Lennox servants only gave the information that the correspondence with the Scottish Queen had been about the restitution of the Lennox estates, not a marriage with Darnley.

Lennox continued to be held in the Tower, and Margaret at Sheen. Elizabeth does not seem to have believed they had any entanglement in de Quadra's scheme. Lennox, still badgered with questions, eventually pointed out that he had freely come to England to serve Henry VIII, and received his lands as a marriage settlement. If the Queen wanted rid of him, she could take back the lands, and send him on his way. This response lacked charm in the eyes of the Council and Elizabeth.

Over the summer, Margaret continued to protest her innocence, admitting only that Darnley's tutor had gone to Scotland, without permission, for which she and Lennox apologised, but no relaxation in their imprisonment was forthcoming. Margaret also began to worry about her finances and that the Lennox estates were not being properly managed.

Then, in autumn of 1562, Elizabeth fell ill with small-pox. She still refused to name a successor, but some of her lords supported the claims of Margaret and Darnley and Lord Robert Dudley suggested that Margaret be freed. Elizabeth recovered, and, after a further deluge of letters from Margaret, agreed to Lennox being released to join his wife at Sheen and then at Syon, but still under house arrest.

Eventually, Elizabeth relented – probably to keep the balance between the various possible successors – Margaret, Queen Mary, or Lady Katherine Grey. It was the Queen's policy to keep them all in suspense. Margaret was required to swear that Darnley would not marry without Elizabeth's consent.

In due course, Elizabeth agreed to promote Lennox's claims to his lands again. For some reason, the Lennoxes seem to have been in poor financial straits, although the vast value of their lands makes this difficult to understand.

Chapter 17: Success

It soon became apparent to Elizabeth's government that a marriage between Mary and Darnley might be the lesser of two evils. Queen Mary was still hoping to marry Don Carlos, the son of Philip of Spain - a far more worrying prospect than marriage with Darnley. Nevertheless, Elizabeth came up with a third option – that Mary should marry Lord Robert Dudley, whom she could rely on to protect her own interests. He was very much against the idea, and Mary was frankly disgusted at the idea she might marry Elizabeth's cast-offs. It is hard to believe that Elizabeth could seriously have thought Mary might agree, even if the pill were sweetened with a promise of the succession to the English Crown.

Darnley was now being paraded at the English court, to encourage Mary to keep in Elizabeth's good books. But Margaret was still hoping that Darnley would be married to Mary, and succeed to Elizabeth's Crown later. This would tend to suggest that she was not looking to overthrow Elizabeth, or she might have preferred Darnley to stay in England. Whilst Elizabeth was still canvassing Dudley as a husband for Mary, the Lennoxes sent their servant, Thomas Fowler, to Scotland to continue negotiations for a match with Darnley. As Don Carlos' mental incapacity was now becoming apparent, it appeared that Mary would not be able to marry him.

Fowler claimed his mission was merely to treat with the Scottish government about Lennox' restoration – to which Queen Mary had finally agreed, supported by her half-brother, the Earl of Moray, who wanted to keep Chatelherault and Arran out of power.

Elizabeth now, for some inexplicable reason, allowed Lennox to travel to Scotland. At first, she refused consent for Darnley to accompany him, but then relented. Meanwhile, Dudley, desperate to avoid being forced to marry Mary himself, was happy to work with Margaret to advance Darnley's hopes.

On 23rd September, 1564, Lennox was received in the Scots Parliament, and the sentence of forfeiture that had hung over him for twenty years was rescinded. Over the next couple of months he was reconciled to his old enemies and had his lands restored. Elizabeth continued to show favour to Darnley – he was permitted, as her nearest male relative, to carry the sword of state in front of her. Elizabeth discussed his merits with Mary's ambassador, and suggested that she was considering putting him forward to Mary as a suitor.

After much vacillation, Elizabeth allowed Darnley to join Lennox in Scotland. She must have known how it would end – was she tired of being badgered on the subject, or had she seen enough of Darnley now to know that Mary would regret marrying him within a very short space of time? The excuse the Lennoxes gave, that Elizabeth professed to accept, was that Darnley was needed about legal matters. He arrived in Scotland in February 1565.

When Mary saw Darnley, now aged twenty, she appears to have liked what she saw, but did not rush into anything. The young man then fell sick, and Mary insisted on visiting him. She was not the first, nor the last, young woman to fall in love with a man lying vulnerable on his sickbed.

In April, Mary wrote to Elizabeth, wishing her to approve a marriage with Darnley, and appoint her as her heir. Elizabeth received the request coldly, and turned on Margaret, ordering her to keep to her rooms. Again the Queen issued conflicting orders, seeming on the one had to encourage the match, and on the other to forbid it.

The Scottish Lords were not thrilled at Mary's choice – the Protestants disliked Darnley as a Catholic, the Hamiltons hated the Lennoxes, and the Douglases wanted to keep Margaret out of the Earldom of Angus. Neither Lennox nor Darnley were endearing themselves – behaving arrogantly and being *'saucier than ever'*. To buy favour from Moray and the Douglas faction, Margaret agreed to give up her claims to Angus.

On hearing that Darnley had accepted the Earldom of Ross (commonly a title given to the sovereign's younger brother) and for which he swore allegiance to Mary, Elizabeth ordered Lennox and Darnley to return to England immediately. They failed to do so and Margaret was sent to the Tower of London.

Chapter 18: The Tower

Margaret was lodged in an upper room, in the Lord Lieutenant's Lodgings, adjacent to the Bell Tower. She had two women and three men servants to attend to her wants and her room was furnished appropriately to her rank. Her younger son, Charles, who was eight, was taken into the household of the Archbishop of York, but not long after returned to his home at Settrington. Temple Newsam and other estates were sequestered – that is, their rents diverted to the Crown, even though they were not formally forfeited.

Margaret continued her interminable letters to Cecil, and also found means to communicate with the French and Spanish Ambassadors, which incensed Elizabeth when she heard of it.

Before long, news reached Elizabeth that Mary and Darnley were married. Darnley, in probably the last circumspect action of his life, forebore attending the nuptial Mass – indicating that he would be sympathetic to the Protestants in Scotland.

Mary and Darnley, now entitled King of Scots, although not invested with the Crown Matrimonial as her first husband had been, requested Elizabeth to release Margaret, promising they had no intention of interfering in England, other than wishing her to have an Act of Parliament passed, investing the succession in them and their heirs, or failing heirs, Margaret's other descendants. In return, they would promise not to change the religion of the country.

Elizabeth, requested by the Kings of France and Spain, as well as Queen Mary, to show mercy to Margaret, refused to sanction her release, but allowed her to be well attended and comfortable in captivity.

Meanwhile, all was not well in the new royal marriage. Darnley was a spoilt, arrogant fool. Mary refused to allow him complete equality with her, and she was also tired of Lennox, who was seeking vengeance on his old enemies. The only thing for which Darnley had proved useful, was his conjugal duty – the Queen was pregnant within a few months of their marriage.

Margaret, presumably, was thrilled. She was also sent a loving letter from her husband, in which he addressed her as his *'sweet Madge'* and told her how much he missed her. Unfortunately, she never received it, as their servant, Fowler, was captured, and the letter confiscated. Fowler was sentenced to death, but released on Queen Mary's request. Her pleas for Margaret, however, were refused.

In Scotland, Mary and Darnley's relationship was going from bad to worse. Concerned over Mary's reliance on her secretary, David Rizzio, Darnley and others of the Scottish Lords (amongst whom Margaret's biographer, Alison Weir includes Lennox, but Darnley's biographer, Caroline Bingham, does not) plotted his murder.

For the first time, so far as is known, Darnley wrote to Elizabeth, asking her to release his mother, saying she had not been party to his marriage to Mary but this too, fell on deaf ears. It was said that, had

Margaret been allowed to travel to Scotland, the problems of Darnley's behaviour would not have arisen. According to the Spanish Ambassador, da Silva, *'she is prudent and brave, and the son respects her more than he does his father.'* Perhaps that was the reason for Elizabeth keeping Margaret under lock and key.

Mary and Darnley had patched up their relationship for public consumption after the Rizzio murder, but, once her son was born, Mary had no further use for him, and nor had any of the nobles of Scotland, except his father. Darnley was murdered in February 1567, certainly with the knowledge of many of the Scots lords and the active involvement of some. Mary's level of complicity, if any, continues to be disputed.

Chapter 19: Grief

When the news reached London of Darnley's death, Elizabeth was sufficiently moved by compassion for Margaret to send Mildred, Lady Cecil, and Margaret, Lady William Howard, (sister-in-law to the Lord Thomas who had been Margaret's first love) to break the news to her. At the time, it was thought that Lennox, too, had been killed, and Margaret was prostrate with grief. Sir William Cecil visited her in person to reassure as to Lennox still being alive, but Margaret was in such a state that Elizabeth was recommended to release her.

Although Margaret and Elizabeth had never been close, the Queen felt genuine compassion, and had Margaret conveyed to Sheen again, where she was reunited with her son, Charles.

Lennox and Margaret were both anxious their son should be avenged, and they believed that the less-than-enthusiastic prosecution of enquiries by Queen Mary indicated her complicity. Lennox harangued Queen Mary, and, with her permission, brought a private prosecution against the Earl of Bothwell, who was acquitted. This was fuel on the fire of the Lennoxes' suspicions.

In April 1567, Lennox returned to England, to try to comfort the grieving Margaret. Many of Elizabeth's courtiers were moved by their sorrow, and suggested that she should ameliorate Margaret's punishment. Eventually, the couple were allowed to live at Coldharbour, one of the lesser London palaces, but the incomes from their estates were still kept in the hands of the Crown.

Despite being strapped for cash, Margaret and Lennox commissioned a painting, known as the *Memorial of Lord Darnley* – of which both the original and an adapted copy survives. Aged 49 and 50, although they were not old, even by Elizabethan standards, the couple were certainly on the cusp of old age, and were concerned they might not live long enough to remind their grandson, James, of the need for vengeance. The painting makes it abundantly clear that they believed Queen Mary to be involved, if not actually the prime mover in the murder.

Margaret and Lennox were not the only people who believed Mary to be guilty, and her marriage, whether willing or not, to Bothwell sealed her fate. She was forced to abdicate in favour of her son, James, Margaret's grandson, and was finally overthrown at the Battle of Langside in 1568. Escaping to England, Mary threw herself on Elizabeth's mercy. Margaret and Lennox were appalled – fearful lest Mary be returned to her throne at the head of an English army. They raced to court and begged Elizabeth for justice. Margaret is described as having a face *'swelled and stained with tears.'*

Initially sympathetic, Elizabeth eventually became fed up with their grief and sent them away, saying they should not believe so great a crime of a Queen without more proof. Mary wrote indignantly to the Queen, complaining that she would see those who accused her of the crime, but would not meet Margaret herself. In Scotland, the baby James was crowned, and his uncle, Mary's illegitimate half-brother, the Earl of Moray, ruled as Regent, bringing James up in the Protestant faith.

Over the next two years Margaret and Lennox continued to proclaim Mary's guilt, but the matter was never resolved. Elizabeth would not take punitive action against an anointed Queen, but nor would she permit Mary to leave captivity. In 1570, the Regent Moray was assassinated. With Scotland in turmoil again, both Margaret and Queen Mary were terrified that something would happen to James. Margaret begged that Elizabeth should have James brought to England, preferably to be brought up by herself. Elizabeth would never have permitted Margaret to have James in her care – first, she would probably have tried to bring him up as a Catholic, and second, with the Queen's nearest male heir in her hands, she might present a danger.

At the same time, Mary wrote to Margaret, saying she had not previously been in correspondence with her, because she was knew that Margaret had been accusing her '*against [her] innocency.*' She asked Margaret's advice on whether James should be sent to England, although she would have preferred him to be sent further afield. Margaret did not (so far as is known) reply, but reiterated her belief in Mary's guilt in a letter to Sir William Cecil.

With Moray dead, there was confusion in Scotland, and a new regent was needed. After some humming and hawing, Elizabeth agreed that Lennox should be sent to Scotland to take over the government – obviously on the proviso that he carried out her instructions to the letter. Margaret and Charles were to stay behind, in London. Whilst no-one would have mentioned the word '*hostage*' there cannot have been any doubt that that was Margaret's role.

Chapter 20: Widowed

Lennox, protesting that he had never thought of being Regent, but was only eager to do Elizabeth's bidding, either as Regent himself, or working with whomever she might appoint, travelled north. He spent as much time as he could with the little king, who was now four years old, and the majority of his correspondence with Elizabeth was via Margaret, the only person he trusted. Unfortunately, the old rivalry with the Hamiltons was not extinguished, and in further feuding, Lennox had some dozen hostages of the Hamiltons hanged. From that moment, he was a marked man. He was on increasingly bad terms with the Earl of Morton – Margaret's first cousin, and the prime mover behind the murder of Secretary Rizzio, back in 1566.

In September of 1571, on the day after Lennox opened the Scots Parliament with his grandson, an armed confrontation took place in the streets of Edinburgh led by the Queen's Party (ie, those favouring the restoration of Mary, which included the Hamiltons). Lennox was killed by a gunshot – possibly by the enemy, but possibly by one of his own ostensible allies – he was not popular even in the King's Party, as, although the Scots Protestants sought English protection, they did not wish to be ruled at second hand by Elizabeth. Two of his last utterances were recorded as – *'if the bairn's* (meaning King James) *well, all's well'*, and a message of love for his *'Sweet Madge'*.

Cecil informed the Queen of Lennox' death, but it was agreed that the matter should be kept quiet until it could be broken to Margaret by Elizabeth herself. Margaret was devastated – she and Lennox had been devoted to each other since their marriage, twenty-six years before.

But Margaret's nature was essentially optimistic and, to use a modern term, pro-active. She never waited for events, but took control where she could. She turned her attention to her remaining child, Lord Charles. He was now about fourteen, and, in her view, lacking a father's discipline.

She also had an eye to his promotion. She therefore asked Cecil (now Lord Burghley) to take him into his household, a frequent way of training young people, and extending their connections.

Burghley refused, but appointed a Protestant tutor for Charles, whom she accepted. Margaret, all the records suggest, remained a Catholic, although many of her friends in her youth – Katherine Suffolk, Mary Richmond and Katherine Parr were Protestant. Lennox had conformed to Protestantism whilst Regent, and Darnley had shown that he could be flexible. It may be that Margaret was that rare creature in sixteenth century Europe, someone tolerant of other religious views.

During this period, Margaret was in close touch with the new regent, the Earl of Mar (who persuaded the Scots Parliament to re-grant the Earldom of Lennox, which had devolved on King James, to her son, Charles). Mar, too, had a short stint in office, although he died of natural causes, and was followed by the Earl of Morton. Morton was later executed for involvement in the death of Darnley, but Margaret either did not know he was involved, or dissembled well – their dealings were always courteous.

A most surprising change in Margaret's views came about in around 1573. In some way, she became (or said she was) convinced that the Queen of Scots was, in fact, innocent of the murder of Lord Darnley. How she was persuaded of this is a mystery. There is no record of the two women meeting, and the extremity of Margaret's earlier accusations make it difficult to imagine what could have passed to change her mind. Nevertheless, the very vehemence of her earlier condemnation also makes it hard to contemplate that she could have pretended to believe in Mary's innocence, if she were not convinced.

Chapter 21: The Last Intrigue

In the late summer of 1573, Margaret requested leave to return to her old home of Settrington. By now, Elizabeth knew that she had been reconciled with Queen Mary, so, although permission was granted, she was told not to go anywhere near Chatsworth, where Mary was being held in the custody of the Earl and Countess of Shrewsbury. The Countess, known to posterity as Bess of Hardwick, had been a friend of Margaret's for at least thirty years. Elizabeth informed Margaret that any visit to Queen Mary might lead people to think they were plotting together. Margaret laughed at such a notion, saying she could never forget the murder of her own child. Whatever the reasons for her change in views on Mary's guilt, she clearly did not intend to share them with Elizabeth.

The following year, Margaret visited travelled north again, to Temple Newsam, this time with Charles, now about nineteen. Not daring to visit Chatsworth, Margaret found an excuse to meet Countess Bess at her home at Rufford Abbey. Conveniently, Bess' daughter, Elizabeth Cavendish, was one of the party. The indulgent and romantic countesses saw that their children had fallen deeply in love, and permitted them to marry. Apparently, any other course would have ended in dishonour (the implication being that Charles and Elizabeth Cavendish had slept together.)

Naturally, there had been no thought of anything more than family joy, despite the fact that Charles was close enough to the throne to require royal permission before marrying. Margaret failed to mention that she had been discussing the marriage with Countess Bess, and her old friend Katherine Willoughby, Duchess of Suffolk, for at least a year. Queen Elizabeth, feeling she had been outwitted once again, sent Margaret back to the Tower.

Margaret must have seen its grey walls almost with a sense of homecoming. She whiled away her time embroidering a handkerchief for Queen Mary with her own hair. Despite diligent searching, Elizabeth's government could not find any evidence of actual treason, other than a marriage without royal consent. There was nothing to suggest a plan to free Mary, or replace Elizabeth, so, eventually, probably by the end of 1575, Margaret was released.

The new Earl and Countess of Lennox were separated, but Lady Lennox gave birth to a daughter, Lady Arbella Stuart.

Unable to influence her grandson's upbringing, Margaret concentrated on Arbella. As further evidence of the rapprochement with Mary, the latter, on drawing up her will in 1577, restored to Margaret her long-lost Earldom of Angus. A futile gesture, as Queen Mary had absolutely no power to put her wishes into effect in Scotland. Margaret, her son, daughter-in-law and grand-daughter, lived quietly in Hackney. Charles had the remittance of the income from the Earldom of Lennox to finance the household, but Margaret had almost nothing of her own.

In 1577, Margaret had the grief of seeing the last of her eight children pre-decease her. She planned a grand tomb for him in Westminster, having him interred at St Augustine, Hackney in the meantime, but was not too busy to correspond with James in Scotland, and oversee the baby Arbella's care until the little girl moved to the home of her other grandmother in 1578. Nevertheless, Margaret still fought on her behalf, requesting the Scots government to recognise Arbella as Countess of Lennox, a plea which was refused. Queen Mary also added a new clause to her aforementioned will, granting the Lennox inheritance to Arbella, but it was of no more value than her grant of Angus to Margaret.

Once again, Margaret succeeded in persuading Elizabeth to help her. The Queen sent a stern letter to the Regent Morton, demanding that Arbella's rights should be recognised – although that might have been to save herself the cost of maintaining Margaret and Arbella – Elizabeth was notably parsimonious.

Margaret made her will in February 1578, presumably feeling her age. She died on either 9th or 10th March, 1578.

Elizabeth footed the bill for the funeral, and permitted it to take place in Westminster Abbey, where she lies still.

Letter from Margaret to Cromwell

This is the letter referenced in Chapter 7.

Transcribed in Footer, Donald W, *Women's Works: 900 - 1550*, 1st edn (New York: Wicked Good Books, 2013) Published by Wicked Words, Editor

My Lord,

What cause have I to give you thanks, and how much bound am I unto you, that by your means hath gotten me, as I trust, the King's Grace's favour again, and besides that, that it pleased you to write and to give me knowledge wherein I might have his Grace's displeasure again (which I pray our Lord sooner to send me death, than that.) I assure you, my Lord, I will never do that thing willingly that should offend his Grace.

And my Lord, whereas it is informed you that I do charge the house (Syon Abbey) with a greater number than is convenient, I assure you I have but two more than I had in the Court, which indeed were Lord Thomas' servants; and the cause that I took them for was for the poverty that I saw them in, and for no other cause else. But seeing, my Lord that it is your pleasure that I shall keep none that did belong unto my Lord Thomas, I will put them from me.

And I beseech you not think that any fancy doth remain in me touching him, but that all my study and care I how to please the King's Grace and to continue in his favour. And my Lord, where it is your pleasure that I shall keep but a few here with me, I trust ye will think that I can have no fewer than I have; for I have but a gentleman and a groom that keeps my apparel, and another that keeps my chamber, and a chaplain that was with me always in the Court.

Now my lord, I beseech you that I may know your pleasure if you would that I should keep any fewer. Howbeit my lord, my servants hath put the house to small charge, fort hey have nothing but the reversion of my board; nor do I call for nothing but that that is given me, howbeit I am very well intreated. And my lord, as for 'resort'. I promise you I have none, except it be gentlewomen that comes to see me, nor never had since I came hither, for if any 'resort' of men had come, it should neither have become me to have seen them, nor yet to have kept them company, being a maid as I am. Now my Lord, I beseech you to be so good as to get my poor servants their wages; and thus I pray our Lord to preserve you, both soul and body.

Letter from Margaret to Angus 15 March 1549

This is the letter referenced in Chapter 12.

My Lorde, after my humble commendacions and desiring of your blessing, this shalbe to signeffye unto you the gret unnaturalnes wiche ye showe me daylye, being to longe to reherse in all poyntes, butt in some I wyll declare nowe laste of all, my Lorde, being nere you, and so desirows to have spoken with you, yet ye refused it and wolde not, where in ye showed your selfe not to be so loving as ye ought to be, or elles so unstable that every body maye turne you, for diverse tymes ye have said you wolde be glad to speyke with your sonne my lorde.

Remember he bathe maryd your owne doughter, and the best chylde to you that ever ye had, if ye call to remembrance your being here in Englande. How be hit,your dedys showethe the forgetfulnes thereof, in so myche as ye ar so contraryto the Kynges majesties affayres, that nowe ys, hys father being so goode and so lyberall a prynce to you, wyche ought neyer to be forgotton ; butt nowe, my lorde, I here saye that ye have professed never to agree with Englande, for so myche as the moost parte of your frendes are slayne. Butt whome can you blame for that butt only youre selfewylles (selfwill), for if ye wolde agre to this godly maryage, (*between Mary Queen of Scots and King Edward VI)* there nedyd no Crjsten blode to be shed.

For Godes sake remember your selfe nowe in your olde age, and seke to have an honorable pease, wiche can not be withowte this marjiage. And what a memoryall shulde that be to you for ever, if ye colde be an instrument for that. If I should wryte so longe a letter as I colde fynde matter with the wrong of your part and the right of myne, hit were to tedyowse for you to rede ; butt for as myche as I purpose, God wylling, to comme to Carlyll shortly after Ester, I wyll kepe it in store to tell you my selfe, for I am sure ye wyll nott refuse commyng to me, all thow my uncle George and the Laideof Dromlaneryk speyke agaynst it, whome I knowe wolde be glad to se you inyour grave, all thowe they flatter you to your face.

My uncle George hathe seid, as dyverse Skottesmen have tolde me, that thowe you had sones he wolde be eyre, and make them all bastardis ; butt, my Lorde, if God sende you no moo sons, and I lyffe after you, he shall have leste parte thereof, or elles many a man shall smarte for it. This leyvinge to declare forther of my mynde tell I maye speyke with you my selfe, I commytte you to the kepinge off All myghty God. whoo sende you longe liffe withe myche honour.

Frome the Kynges magestyes castell of Wreyssell, the xvth daye of Marche,

Be your humble doughter,

Margrett Lennox.

Aspects of Lady Margaret Douglas' Life

Chapter 22: The Devonshire Manuscript

In Henry VIII's youth, his romantic streak had been given expression with jousts and tournaments, at which his immense physical prowess had let him excel, but by the time Lady Margaret Douglas came to court to serve Queen Anne Boleyn, the King was in his mid-forties and there were fewer jousts. The young men of the court, rather than wooing their ladies with feats of arms, took to writing music and extravagant verse.

The conventions of the game were clearly laid down in Baldassare Castiglione's 'The Book of the Courtier', an Italian work, published in the early sixteenth century, and known in the courts of Italy and France, which heavily influenced England – although an English edition was not published until 1561. Gentlemen sighed over unattainable ladies, who treated them with disdain, or flirted with them, with no intention of delivering on the promise.

Chief amongst the poets of the court were the Queen's brother, George Boleyn, Viscount Rochford; her cousin, Henry Howard, Earl of Surrey, (brother of Lady Margaret's friend Mary Howard, Duchess of Richmond) and Sir Thomas Wyatt, a childhood friend of Anne and George, and once Anne's suitor. Many of the other ladies and gentlemen, including the King himself, wrote verse too, varying in skill from the completely dreadful, to the barely adequate.

One of the fashionable styles was the 'verse conversation'. A poem would be written down and shared amongst friends, with each adding an answer to the previous poem. A large group of verses is contained in a manuscript, now known as the Devonshire Manuscript, a collection of 185 poems plus a further eleven fragments of writing or anagrams. The manuscript itself is quarto sized – that is, a single sheet folded to make four pages, and then bound. In all, the book has 114 leaves. It seems likely the book was originally owned by Mary Howard (her married initials, MF for Mary FitzRoy, are on it).

Of these verses, the vast majority have been attributed to Sir Thomas Wyatt, with other items by the Earl of Surrey, Mary Shelton, Sir Edmund Knyvett and other members of the court, and a later one, to Henry, Lord Darnley, Margaret's son. A group have been attributed to Lord Thomas Howard and Lady Margaret Douglas.

The number of poems ascribed to Lord Thomas and to Margaret differs between scholars. As many as thirteen, and as few as three, have been attributed to him, and nine and two respectively to her. She appears to have transcribed 16 of them and annotated at least 50 of the pages, with comments such as '*and this*' or '*learn but to sing it*'. The other main transcriber appears to be Mary Shelton, whose name appears in an acrostic verse. Occasionally Margaret and Mary differ on their view of the worthiness of poems – Margaret writes on one '*forget this*' and Mary replies '*it is worthy.*'

The difficulty, of course, is knowing which of the poems Howard and Margaret actually composed, and which they merely transcribed. There is a group that appear to relate to the period when the couple were in the Tower of London, sent there as punishment for their unsanctioned betrothal. We must assume, if they were contemporaneous with that, that they sent poems back and forth between them (the individual poems were not entered sequentially). This is not impossible, as imprisonment for nobility, although onerous as a loss of freedom, was not usually repressive in itself.

In one poem he writes:

'There is no care for cure of mind
But to forget (which cannot be!)
I cannot sail against the wind,
Nor help the thing past remedy.'

In a later (probably) verse, the first and last stanzas of six are:

'Thy promise was to love me best
And that thy heart with mine should rest
And not to break this, thy behest –
Thy promise was, thy promise was.
...
But since to change thou dost delight
And that thy faith has ta'en his flight
As thou deservest, I shall the 'quite [requite]
I promise thee, I promise thee.'

Margaret's compositions include:

'...And though that I be banished him fro'
His speech, his sight and company,
Yet will I, in spite of his foe,
Him love and keep my fantasy

Do what they will, and do their worst
(for all they do is vanity)
For asunder my heart shall burst
Surer than change my fantasy'

The poems attributed to Howard bespeak his own faithfulness, and his depression when he discovers that Margaret has given up all thought of him. As she said to Cromwell, she no longer had '*any fancy thereunto.*' Whether her renunciation is genuine, is another question. The shadow of the axe is not conducive to romance.

One poem ascribed to her, suggests that, far from forgetting Lord Thomas, she grieved sincerely over his death, to the point of feeling suicidal:

'Wherefore, sweet father, I you pray,
Bear this my death with patience
And torment not your hairs grey
But freely pardon mine offence
Sith't [since it] proceeded of love's fervency
And of my heart's constancy
Lett me not [do not keep me from] from the sweet presence
Of him that I have caused to die.'

We need to be careful about inferring the actual feelings of Thomas Howard and Margaret Douglas from the poems, which reflect the conventions of courtly love, yet the Devonshire Manuscript gives a rare glimpse into the amusements and tastes of the young men and women of the 1530s.

Mary Howard would remain Margaret's friend until her own death in 1557, despite the widening gap in religion between them. Mary Shelton married Sir Anthony Heveningham in about 1540, and, later, Sir Philip Appleyard, dying in 1571.

Chapter 23: The Will of Lady Margaret Douglas

Lady Margaret Douglas' will makes interesting reading, and tells us a bit about Margaret, her relationships with her servants and also with two of the most important figures at Elizabeth's court, Sir William Cecil, Lord Burghley, and Robert Dudley, Earl of Leicester.

Margaret made the will in the spring of 1578 (although she dated it 1577, as old style dating was still in use). By this time, all her children had died, and she had only two grand-children, James VI, King of Scots, and Lady Arbella Stuart. She had urged the Scots government to recognise Lady Arbella as Countess of Lennox, but the Regent of Scotland, the Earl of Morton, had refused, and the lands and revenues of the earldom had reverted to King James.

At the time of her death, Margaret was living in Hackney, a country suburb on the edge of the City of London. Although the extensive lands that had been settled on Margaret and her husband, Matthew Stuart, Earl of Lennox, had not formally been confiscated, as despite various periods of imprisonment, no actual charges had been brought against them, the income and control had been sequestered by the government. Only her lands at Settrington in Yorkshire were in her hands, or those of her appointees.

For a woman who was the daughter of a queen-consort, half-sister of a king, and close friend of a sovereign Queen, as well as mistress of an estate third only to that of the Crown in the north of England, Margaret had surprisingly little to leave.

As was customary, she began by bequeathing her soul to Almighty God. She chose to be buried in Westminster Abbey – this is, in itself, Margaret's clearest statement of her belief in her royal lineage and the claim to the throne of England that she passed on to her descendants. Her beloved husband, Matthew, Earl of Lennox, had been buried in Scotland, following his assassination, but she chose to lie with her mother's family – the Tudors.

Westminster Abbey was the burial place of her grand-parents, Henry VII and Elizabeth of York, her cousin, Mary I, and her other cousin,

Frances Brandon, Duchess of Suffolk. In due course, Elizabeth I, James VI & I and Mary, Queen of Scots (Margaret's niece) would all lie there. It seems that Elizabeth had no objection to Margaret being interred in the royal chapel, and in fact, ended up paying for the ceremony, as Margaret's possessions could not cover her debts and funeral expenses.

Margaret's grandson, James VI, received her new black velvet bed. This seems rather a bizarre bequest, but beds and their furnishings were extremely expensive, and a status symbol. Bed chambers were more public than they are now, and it was perfectly normal for guests to be received there. A smart set of hangings for the bed was important. Black velvet, too, was very pricey.

Her next major bequest is that of her sheep to Thomas Fowler – again, somewhat surprising to think of a Countess noting her sheep, but they were probably the next most valuable thing she owned, and great ladies in the sixteenth century were closer to estate management than their Victorian counterparts. Margaret clearly trusted Thomas Fowler, although there are indications in other records that he was actually reporting on her activities to both Burghley and Leicester – it is difficult to be sure, as factors, stewards and other senior servants often worked for several people – employment not being so fixed as it now is. He had certainly been instrumental in organising the match between Darnley and Mary.

Margaret also left Fowler her collection of clocks, watches and dials. Clocks, too were extremely valuable and fashionable items, only becoming indoor, table-top pieces, such as we now have, in the final quarter of the fifteenth century, when the spring mechanism was invented. They were often owned by kings or nobles as manifestations of wealth and sophistication. This mention of a collection of time-pieces, together with a comment on Margaret in the 1550s, that she had amassed many relics and icons, suggests that she had the nature of a collector.

Leaving items of such value to Fowler, implies a warmer relationship beyond the fact that she owed him money. Her trust in him is indicated by his appointment as her executor.

As well as executors, it was usual to name overseers of a will. Margaret chose the two most powerful men in Elizabethan England – William Cecil, Lord Burghley, Elizabeth's closest counsellor and Lord Treasurer, and Robert Dudley, Earl of Leicester, the Queen's closest male friend. These two men had been the recipients of many letters from Margaret, usually relating to requests from her to speak favourably of her to the Queen, but we can probably infer that they were also her friends. Burghley's wife, Mildred Cecil, had been one of the ladies sent to break the news of Darnley's death.

Leicester had promoted Margaret as a possible successor to Elizabeth in the early 1560s, rather than the more Protestant candidate, Lady Katherine Grey, and it was with Leicester (amongst others) that Margaret had dined three days before her death. Her bequest to him of her pomander beads, as well as of her '*tablet*' of Henry VIII, suggests a personal affection. A tablet might be a small book, or a picture.

Finally, her jewels were to be given to her grand-daughter, the Lady Arbella, on her marriage, or when she attained the age of fourteen. So far as is known, these jewels did not include the famous Lennox Jewel, although there is no inventory, so we cannot be sure.

It seems that Arbella did not receive her bequest. In 1590, there was a request to King James to release goods seized from the estate of Thomas Fowler, in satisfaction of a debt to the Earl of Lennox.

'Sundrie tymes I have moved the King and Lord Chancelour that the jewelles late in the handes of Thomas Fowler, deceased, and appertayning to the Lady Arbell, might be restored to her.'

Margaret's most important legacy, however, was her royal blood – it was a positive legacy for James, but caused Lady Arbella to live a sad and constrained life.

An Excerpt from the Will of Margaret, Countess of Lennox.

This transcript is taken from North Country Wills, published by the Surtees Society

I, Margaret, Countesse of Lennox, widowe, late wife of Mathewe, Erle of Lennox, Regent of Scotlande, deceased, the six and twentieth daye of Februarie, 1577.

My bodie to be buried in the greate churche of Westminster, in the monument sepulture or tombe alreadie bargeyned for, and appointed to be made and sett uppe in the saide churche.

Also I will that the bodie of my sonne Charles shalbe removed from the churche of Hackney, and laide with myne both in one vawte or tombe in the saide churche of Westminster. And I give for my buriall the somme of twelve hundred poundes alias one thowsande twoo hundred poundes to be made and furnished of my plate, howshouldstuffe, and move ables to be soulde therefore And I will that fourtie poundes of the saide twelve hundred poundes shalbe given to the poore people at the daie of my buriall, and that there be one hundred gownes furnished to a hundred poore women.

Also I give to the Kinge of Skottes for a remembraunce of me, his grandmother, my newe fielde bed of blacke velvet imbrodered with flowers of neadle worke with the furniture thereunto belonginge, as curteins, quilte, and bedsteed, but not aine other beddinge there unto.

Also I give to Margaret Wilton my woman fiftie poundes, and to everie other servant one yeares wages.

To Thomas Fowler my servaunte all my stocke of sheepe in the custodie of Lawrence Nessebett, Symonde Doddesworthe, and Rowland Fothergyll, within my lordshippe of Settrington, in the countie of Yorke, beinge in numbre eight hundred, at six scoare to the hundred.

And where I owe unto the saide Thomas Fowler seaven hundred threscore eightene poundes and fiftene shillings uppon the determinacon of his last aecompte, I will the same somme be paide of my goodes, chattells, plate, and jewells.

Also I give to the saide Thomas Fowler all my clockes, watches, dials.

And I make John Kaye, of Hackney, esquire, and the saide Thomas Fowler my executors.

And I give the saide John Kaye fourtie powndes, and I will my verie good lordes, William, Lorde Burghley, Lord Treasawrer of Englande, and Roberte, Earle of Leicester my overseers.

And I give to them for theire paines, viz. to the Lord Treasurer my ringe with fowre diamondes sett square therein, blacke enamiled, and to the Earle of Leycester

my chaine of pommaunder beades netted over with golde, and my tablett with the picture of Kinge Henrye the eighte therein.

All the reste of my jewells, goodes, I give to the Ladye Arabell, daughter of my sonne Charles, deceased.

Lady Margaret's Will in Modern English

Tudor Times translation with our notes in brackets.

I, Margaret, Countess of Lennox, widow, late wife of Matthew, Earl of Lennox, Regent of Scotland, deceased the six and twentieth day of February, 1577 (*old style, 1578 in modern dating*) My body to be buried in the great church of Westminster, (*Westminster Abbey*) in the monument, sepulchre or tomb already bargained for and appointed to be made and set up in the said church.

Also I will that the body of my son Charles (Lord Charles Stuart, 1st (*sometimes notated as 5th*)Earl of Lennox shall be removed from the church of Hackney, and laid with mine both in one vault or tomb in the said church of Westminster.

And I give for my burial the sum of twelve hundred pounds, alias one thousand two hundred pounds to be made and furnished of my plate, household stuff, and movables to be sold therefore. And I will that forty pounds of the said twelve hundred pounds shall be given to the poor people at the day of my burial, and that there be one hundred gowns furnished to a hundred poor women.

Also I give to the King of Scots (*James VI*) for a remembrance of me, his grandmother, my new field bed of black velvet, embroidered with flowers of needle work with the furniture thereunto belonging, as (*that is*) curtains, quilt, and bedstead, but not any other bedding there unto.

Also I give to Margaret Wilton my woman fifty pounds, and to every other servant one year's wages.

To Thomas Fowler my servant all my stock of sheep in the custody of Lawrence Nisbet, Simon Doddsworth and Rowland Fothergill, my lordship of Settrington, in the county of York, being in number eight hundred, at six score to the hundred (*ie 1000 sheep in total*).

And where I owe unto the said Thomas Fowler seven hundred threescore eighteen pounds and fifteen shillings (*£778 15s.*) upon the determination of his last account, I will the same sum be paid of my goods, chattels, plate, and jewels.

Also I give to the said Thomas Fowler all my clocks, watches, dials.

And I make John Kaye, of Hackney, esquire, and the said Thomas Fowler my executors.

And I give the said John Kaye forty pounds, and I will my very good lords, William (*Cecil*), Lord Burghley, Lord Treasurer of England, and Robert (*Dudley*) Earl of Leicester my overseers. And I give to them for their pains (trouble), viz. to the Lord Treasurer my ring with four diamonds set square therein, black enamelled, and to the Earl of Leicester my chain of pomander beads netted over with gold, and my tablet (possibly a book or a small picture) with the picture of King Henry the eighth (Margaret's uncle) therein.

All the rest of my jewels, goods, I give to the Lady Arabell (*Lady Arbella Stuart*), daughter of my son Charles, deceased.

The will was proved on 27th March 1578 (*New style dating*) by Thomas Fowler. The other executor renounced his role.

Chapter 24: Following the Footsteps of Margaret Douglas

Lady Margaret spent her childhood in Scotland and the borders before being housed in the palaces of the English court. During her married life, she spent the majority of her time in the great houses that Henry VIII had granted her – that is, when she was not in the Tower of London.

The numbers in the text below correspond to those on the map which follows.

*

Margaret was born in the English border castle of Harbottle (1), Northumberland. Today, Harbottle is quiet and isolated, it seems that nothing more exciting than lambing and shearing the hardy upland sheep could ever have happened here, but in 1515 things were very different.

The Anglo-Scots border was the scene of conflict for hundreds of years, between the kings, the kings and their rebellious subjects and between the border families who preyed on each other and on passing travellers. Reivers, they were called, and a spot of sheep or cattle rustling seems rather romantic in retrospect, but, for the people of the time, the screams in the night, the smoke from burn-out villages and farmsteads and the constant fear of blackmail (protection money, rather than the modern form) were a depressing fact of life. Loyalty was to clan, rather than king, and some of the most notorious families, such as the Armstrongs, refused to heed the laws of either country.

Because violence was endemic and insoluble, when the countries were not formally at war, there was a system of regular meeting days to resolve issues and offer redress where possible. These days were managed by the Wardens of the West, East and Middle marches for both countries. There are copious letters from the various wardens complaining that the other side had not turned up, or had refused redress, or wouldn't hand over stolen goods, or hostages as agreed, but generally, unless either king were seeking an excuse for war, the matters were managed locally.

So far as can be inferred from the letters, it seems that, whilst the Scots did more raiding over the border into England, the English Kings and their wardens spent more time and money deliberately undermining the Scottish government and suborning loyalties. Neither side comes out with any credit. For the Scots Kings, to be seen to dispense justice in the borders was an important part of their role, and James IV and V and Mary all presided over *'Justices in Eyre'* personally.

Such was the situation when Margaret, Dowager Queen of Scots, dashed over the border to Harbottle, where she and her baby stayed for some months before heading, via Morpeth, Durham and Newcastle for London. On arrival in the English capital, Lady Margaret, too young to know where she was, spent time at Barnard's castle, Greenwich Palace and Scotland Yard (where during the mediaeval period, the Scottish kings visiting or held hostage in England, were housed).

Returning to Scotland, aged eighteen months, Margaret spent her childhood in the royal palaces of Stirling (2), Edinburgh Castle and Holyrood Palace. She would also have spent significant amounts of time at Tantallon Castle (3).

Tantallon, one of the most impressive castles in the Scottish Lowlands, clings to the cliffs opposite the notorious Bass Rock. On a sunny day, it is an impressive sight; on a stormy day, it is a fearful one. Tantallon was almost impregnable, and James V failed to subdue it when he was attempting to capture Margaret's father, Archibald Douglas, 6th Earl of Angus in 1528. Margaret may have been there at the time, but was more likely to have been at Coldingham Priory.

At some point Margaret was sent into England for safety, and perhaps for her value as a hold over her half-brother, King James, and her mother, the Dowager Queen. She went first to Norham Castle (4), another border fortress, actually on the River Tweed, where she could see out to Scotland, and later at Berwick Castle, England's outpost on the north side of the Tweed. After some months there, Margaret was sent south. She may have gone to her aunt, Mary, the French Queen, at Westhorpe in Suffolk, or straight to the English court, and the household of her cousin, the Princess Mary. The English court spent most of its time during the late 1520s at Greenwich and Richmond, with the Princess at Beaulieu and Hunsdon.

In the 1530s, Margaret was in the retinue of Anne Boleyn, often at Hampton Court and at the new palace of Whitehall (5), being constructed from the old palace of the Archbishops of York. It was at Whitehall that she agreed to marry Lord Thomas Howard. For this misdemeanour of engaging herself without royal consent, she was dispatched to the Tower of London (6) where she spent anything between six and fifteen months in the period from July 1536. This was followed by a period at Syon Abbey (8), which was not dissolved until 1539.

She had left Syon by June 1538, returning probably to the house of the Princess, now demoted to '*Lady*', Mary. In 1539, Margaret was named as one of the great ladies in attendance on Anne of Cleves, and she was present at the new Queen's entry to the capital at Blackheath. For the next few months, she was with the court at Hampton Court, Greenwich, Whitehall and Westminster. When Henry divorced Queen Anne to marry Katheryn Howard, (an event which took place at Oatlands Palace) Margaret remained in the royal household, probably in the same position as first of the Great Ladies. When Katheryn Howard's star crashed miserably to earth, Margaret was also reprimanded for '*lightness*' of behaviour – she had been conducting a flirtation with Charles Howard, the Queen's brother.

With no Queen, there was no role for ladies at court so Margaret spent the period between November 1541 and July 1542 largely at Kenninghall (9) in Norfolk, not far from where her lover, Lord Thomas Howard, who had not survived his sojourn in the Tower, was buried at Thetford. The palace of Kenninghall has long disappeared but in Margaret's day was a splendid late mediaeval structure, built in the period 1505-1525, and owned by the Duke of Norfolk. Margaret may well have been happy there, in the company of her friend, Mary, Duchess of Richmond.

In July 1543, she was back at Hampton Court where she witnessed the marriage of Henry VIII to his sixth wife, Katherine Parr. For the next year, she was in attendance on the Queen, then eleven months later, Margaret herself was married.

Her husband, Matthew Stuart, 4th Earl of Lennox, and she were granted huge estates in the north of England. Her first child was born in London, at Stepney Palace, but her second at Temple Newsam (10), near Leeds. Temple Newsam, originally owned by the Knights Templar, had been confiscated from Thomas, Lord Darcy, for his part in the Pilgrimage of Grace. Today, it is an extremely imposing Jacobean mansion, built in red brick in the traditional 'U' shape around a courtyard – it is so imposing, it has been called the 'Hampton Court of the North'. The majority of the current building post-dates Margaret's residence, but part of the main block is still the original Tudor house she knew. Her son, the ill-fated Lord Darnley, was born here on 7th December 1545. It is now owned by Leeds City Council and contains an extensive art collection.

Temple Newsam wasn't the only great house the Lennoxes owned. They were granted the lands of Jervaulx Abbey (11) and built an extremely impressive mansion there, within the Abbey walls. They also had a manor at Settrington (12), in North Yorkshire, also confiscated from one of the rebels of the Pilgrimage of Grace, Sir Francis Bigod. Margaret spent much of her time here during Elizabeth's reign, as far away from court and as close to the coast as possible, to allow her to send messages and letters to France, Spain and Scotland with minimum chance of interception.

Wressle Castle, once the property of the Percy Earls of Northumberland, was another of the Lennoxes' properties. Now an impressive ruin, it was from Wressle that Margaret dated a letter to her father, the Earl of Angus, in which she tells him how angry she is that he has disinherited her. Wressle is close to the Humber, and, at that time, passage to London or Edinburgh from there would have been as easy by ship as by road, although we don't know if Margaret ever travelled by ship herself.

Margaret's life was devoted to the promotion of her two sons, and she went to extreme lengths to promote Lord Darnley's marriage to Mary, Queen of Scots, even suffering a long imprisonment in the Tower, when Elizabeth found out.

Not chastened by this experience, nor by Darnley's death, she continued to try to promote her family, even without royal consent. In 1574 she visited an old friend, Elizabeth (Bess) Hardwick, Countess of Shrewsbury. Elizabeth Shrewsbury was enormously rich, with a daughter, and Margaret had a second son whose veins were rich in royal blood.

Lady Shrewsbury and her husband were also the gaolers of Margaret's niece and daughter-in-law, Mary, Queen of Scots. Whilst Margaret did not dare so far to defy the Queen as to visit Queen Mary, she did visit Lady Shrewsbury at Rufford Abbey (13), and it was here that the two ladies were amazed to discover that their children had fallen so far in love, that the only honourable thing to do was to let them marry at once, even without royal permission. Rufford is currently in the care of English Heritage, and there is quite an extensive range of buildings to see, although they are not habitable. Margaret had another taste of the Tower for this unapproved marriage.

Towards the end of her life, Margaret spent most of her time in Hackney (14) a fashionable area of east London, and it was there that she died on 9th March, 1578. There is no trace now of Margaret's house, although the church tower of St Augustine remains, and can be visited on the first Sunday of each month. Hackney was a particularly popular area with Catholic recusants, and that might have influenced Margaret's choice of location.

Margaret was buried in Westminster Abbey (15), in the Lady Chapel built by her grandfather, Henry VII. On the accession to the English Crown of her grandson, James VI of Scotland, he had an impressive new monument built for her.

Key to Map

1. Harbottle Castle, Northumberland
2. Stirling Castle, Stirling, Scotland
3. Tantallon Castle, North Berwick, Scotland
4. Norham Castle, Northumberland
5. Berwick Castle, Northumberland
6. Whitehall, London
7. Tower of London
8. Syon Abbey, Greater London
9. Kenninghall, Norfolk
10. Temple Newsam, Leeds
11. Jervaulx Abbey, Yorkshire
12. Settrington, Yorkshire
13. Rufford Abbey, Nottinghamshire
14. Hackney, London
15. Westminster Abbey, London

Chapter 25: Book Review

Lady Margaret Douglas has been largely neglected in Tudor historiography. She does, however, play an important part in Leanda de Lisle's *Tudor: The Family Story* as the link between the Tudors and Stuarts.

Tudor: The Family Story

Author: Leanda de Lisle

Publisher: Chatton & Winus

In a nutshell An ambitious panorama across the wider Tudor family, introducing the reader to some figures less well-known than Henry VIII and his wives.

Many histories of the Tudor period start with Henry Tudor, erstwhile Earl of Richmond, springing into life as he lands at Milford in South Wales, ready to capture the Crown. This book begins sixty years before and shows the progress of the Tudors from dispossessed gentry of Wales after the failure of Owain Glyndwr's attempts to throw off English control, to half-brothers of the King, and finally to the Crown. This was achieved first through the clandestine marriage of Owen Tudor to the widowed Queen, Catherine de Valois, then the marriage of their son, Edmund, into a junior member of the Lancastrian branch of the royal family – Margaret Beaufort.

Margaret Beaufort is only the first of the dominating female figures of the Tudor family whom Ms de Lisle shows as using all the weapons available to women when direct power for a female was rare: money, connections, intrigue and the sheer inability of men to contemplate that women might have more complex lives than their outward show of wifely obedience might suggest.

One of the curses of the Tudor family was the tendency of the men to die young: Prince Arthur; Henry Fitzroy; Edward VI; Henry, Earl of Lincoln and Charles, Earl of Lennox all died as young men, and many others in infancy. This left a plethora of female heirs in an era uncomfortable with feminine rule. De Lisle traces some of these young women, the Grey sisters, Lady Margaret Clifford, and Lady Arbella Stuart, through lives often made more dangerous, but never happier, through their proximity to the throne. Ms de Lisle skilfully weaves these characters in and out of the main narrative which follows the five (or six, if Lady Jane Grey is counted) monarchs as they quarrelled amongst themselves, and tried to isolate their heirs.

One of the most interesting facets of Ms de Lisle's writing, is her challenge to perceptions of history that have been conditioned by propaganda developed by later generations – good examples are the view of Frances Brandon, Duchess of Suffolk and mother of Lady Jane Grey as little better than a child-abuser, which has no basis in contemporary records; the inclination of Mary I to spare Lady Jane, shown here as a clever political ploy, in the wider context of religious turmoil, only foiled by the intriguing of Lady Jane's father; and the re-evaluation of Lady Margaret Douglas' relationship with Henry VIII, freed from the 'spin' of her enemies.

Necessarily, in a work of this vast scope, not everything can be covered, and there are some tantalising glimpses of other characters whom it would be interesting to learn more about, such as the elusive Lady Eleanor Brandon and her daughter, Lady Margaret Clifford, and Lord Strange and his siblings and children.

An elegantly written narrative which gives context to the Tudor century – highly recommended.

Bibliography

Accounts of the Treasurer of Scotland: v. 5-8:. Edinburgh: H.M. General Register House, 1877

Calendar of State Papers: Domestic Series: Edward VI, 1547-1553. United Kingdom: Stationery Office Books.

Calendar of State Papers: Domestic: Mary I 1553-1558. London: Public Record Office.

Calendar of State Papers Simancas, British History Online (HMSO, 1892) Hume, Martin A S, ed.,

Calendar of State Papers: Venice <http://www.british-history.ac.uk/cal-state-papers/venice/vol2/vii-lxi> [accessed 7 October 2015]

Cecil Papers, http://www.british-history.ac.uk/cal-cecil-papers (Accessed: 7 September 2015)

Cotton. MS Caligula, B III. Fol 273. (n.d.).

Cotton MS Caligula B II Fol. 283. (n.d.).

Cotton MS Caligula B VI Fol 119b'

Cotton MS Vesp F XIII Fol. 138 (n.d)

Letters and Papers, Foreign and Domestic, of the Reign of Henry VIII: Preserved in the Public Record Office, the British Museum, and Elsewhere in England (United Kingdom: British History Online, 2014) https://www.british-history.ac.uk/letters-papers-hen8/ Brewer, John Sherren, and James Gairdner

Ambassdes de Messieurs de Noailles En Anglettere, 5 vols., 1783

Alford, Stephen, *Burghley: William Cecil at the Court of Elizabeth I* (London: Yale University Press, 2008)

Bingham, Caroline, *Darnley: A Life of Henry Stuart, Lord Darnley, Consort of Mary Queen of Scots* (London: Constable, 1995)

Borman, Tracy, *Thomas Cromwell: The Untold Story of Henry VIII's Most Faithful Servant* (United Kingdom: Hodder & Stoughton, 2014)

Brigden, Susan, *Thomas Wyatt: The Heart's Forest*, 1st edn (London: Faber and Faber, 2012)

De Lisle, Leanda, *Tudor: The Family Story* (United Kingdom: Chatto & Windus, 2013)

Drummond, William, ed., *The History of Scotland from the Year 1423 until the Year 1542, Containing the Lives and Reigns of James I, II, III, IV and V* (London: H Hills for R Tomlins and himself, 1655)

Durant, David N. *Bess of Hardwick: Portrait of an Elizabethan Dynast*, 1st edn (London: Weidenfield and Nicolson, 1977).

Ellis, Henry, *Original Letters, Illustrative of English History: Including Numerous Royal Letters: From Autographs in the British Museum, the State Paper Office, and One or Two Other Collections.*, 1st edn (New York: Printed for Harding, Triphook, & Lepard, 1824)

Footer, Donald *Women's Works: 900 - 1550*, 1st edn (New York: Wicked Good Books, 2013)

Foxe, John, *The Acts and Monuments of John Foxe: A New and Complete Edition: With a Preliminary Dissertation by the Rev. George Townsend* (London: R.R. Seeley and W. Burnside, 1837)

Fraser, Antonia, *Mary Queen of Scots* (London: HarperCollins Publishers, 1970)

Fraser, William, *The Douglas Book*, 4 vols. (Edinburgh, 1885)

Hall, Edward, *Hall's Chronicle.* (S.l.: Ams Press, 1909)

Hayward, Maria, ed., *The Great Wardrobe Accounts of Henry VII and Henry VIII* (United Kingdom: London Record Society, 2012)

Holinshed, Raphael, *Holinshed's Chronicles of England, Scotland & Ireland* (United Kingdom: AMS Press, 1997)

Lemon, Robert, ed., *Calendar of State Papers: Domestic Series: Edward, Mary and Elizabeth*, British History Online (London: HMSO, 1856)

Leslie, John, *The History of Scotland: From the Death of King James I, in the Year 1436 to 1561* (United States: Kessinger Publishing, 2007)

Marshall, Rosalind Kay, *Queen Mary's Women: Female Relatives, Servants, Friends and Enemies of Mary, Queen of Scots* (Edinburgh: John Donald Publishers, 2006)

Morse H., *Select Documents Of English Constitutional History*, ed. by George Burton Adams and Morse H Stephens (United States: Kessinger Publishing, 2007)

Perry, Maria, *Sisters to the King*, 2nd edn (Andre Deutsch, 2002)

Porter, Linda, *Crown of Thistles: The Fatal Inheritance of Mary Queen of Scots* (United Kingdom: Macmillan, 2013)

Porter, Linda, *Katherine the Queen: The Remarkable Life of Katherine Parr*, Kindle (Macmillan, 2010)

Shulman, Nicola, *Graven with Diamonds: The Many Lives of Thomas Wyatt: Courtier, Poet, Assassin, Spy* (London: Short Books, 2011)

Strickland, Agnes: *Lives Of The Queens Of Scotland And English Princesses: Connected With The Regal Succession Of Great Britain* (Harper & Brothers, 1859), i & ii

Starkey, David, *Six Wives of Henry VIII* (London: Vintage, 2004)

Weir, Alison, *Elizabeth, the Queen,* Kindle (London: Random House UK, 2009)

Weir, Alison, *The Lost Tudor Princess* (London: Jonathan Cape 2015)

Whitelock, Anna, *Elizabeth's Bedfellows,* Kindle (London: Bloomsbury Publishing plc, 2013)

Whitelock, A. (2010) *Mary Tudor: princess, bastard, queen.* 1st edn. New York: Random House Publishing Group.

www.tudortimes.co.uk

28462077R00054

Printed in Great Britain
by Amazon